A Student's Guide to Studying Psychology

Thomas M. Heffernan
School of Social Sciences
University of Teesside

Psychology Press
a member of the Taylor & Francis group

Copyright © 1997 by Psychology Press
an imprint of Erlbaum (UK) Taylor & Francis Ltd.

Psychology Press, Publishers
27 Church Road
Hove
East Sussex, BN3 2FA
UK

British Library Cataloguing in Publication Data

A catalogue record for this book is available from the British Library

ISBN 0-86377-472-5 (Hbk)
ISBN 0-86377-473-3 (Pbk)

Cover design by Joyce Chester
Printed and bound in the UK by Biddles Ltd., Guildford and King's Lynn

*Dedicated to the memory of my mother,
Mary Heffernan*

Contents

5. A guide to preparing for examinations   91

6. After the degree: Opportunities for a graduate of psychology   103

Preface

The impetus for writing this book comes from years of teaching on undergraduate courses in psychology and from listening to students themselves. Throughout those years, consistent weaknesses in student work has been evident in those aspects of studying that are crucial skills in getting a student through a degree course, and for achieving the best possible degree classification at the end of the course. As competition for places on postgraduate courses, and in the general "careers market", increases, achieving the best possible grades (and subsequent degree classification) can be crucial.

This text represents a practical guide to studying psychology at an undergraduate level, as well as at pre-degree level (e.g. on an Access course). The text will also be of use to those who are seriously thinking about studying psychology, but have not yet applied. Undergraduate students often complain of not knowing what is expected of them in terms of the reports or essays they write, how to study during lectures, for seminars, etc., and how to prepare effectively for examinations. It is expected that this guide will be of practical use to students of psychology by providing a concise set of guides in a easy to follow format.

Chapter 1 is an introduction to psychology, explaining how psychology as an academic subject differs from the layperson's view of it, and it provides an overview of the major perspectives within psychology, demonstrating the multi-disciplinary nature of the subject. Chapter 2 focuses on what different modes of presentation there are on a psychology course—lectures, seminars, tutorials—and provides concise, practical guidelines on how best to approach these. Chapter 3 comprises a study guide on essay writing and referencing skills. Chapter 4 is a guide to research methods in psychology, ethics in research, and empirical research report writing. Together, essay writing and report writing will make up the bulk of a student's work on a psychology course. Chapter 5 contains good advice on how best to revise for examinations and useful tips on taking an exam. Finally, Chapter 6 provides advice on what to do on completion of an undergraduate psychology degree. This final chapter considers what it means to have graduate status; it covers postgraduate study and applied areas of psychology, as well as other applications. The final chapter also provides advice on writing a curriculum vitae (cv).

The main emphasis of this text is on providing good practical advice on major aspects related to studying on a psychology course. It is expected that existing students of psychology, as well as those who are considering studying psychology as an academic subject, will benefit from this book.

I am very grateful to the following people for their feedback on this book: Rebecca Coates, Colin Hamilton, Renee Harding, and Lin Norton; and to the following people for their contributions to the book: Neil McLaughlin Cook, Keith Morgan, and Sue Thomas. Finally, I should like to express my thanks to my wife, Anne, for all her support.

CHAPTER ONE

Introduction to psychology

WHAT IS PSYCHOLOGY?

To the layperson, the term "Psychology" might mean something like "the study of people" or "the study of the mind", both of which are correct but a little vague. A more formal definition of psychology would be *the scientific study of human mental processes, motivations, and behaviour*. Animal research is also conducted so that comparisons can be made between animal and human behaviour—from which many models of behaviour have been developed (Pinel, 1996). During its development, psychology has undergone a number of changes. One of these changes is a greater reliance on the scientific method. This means the use of scientific techniques, approaches, designs, and analyses, all of which allow the psychologist to study and interpret a range of human behaviour systematically, and predict or control it with some precision (Solso & Johnson, 1994). The use of systematic study allows us to test long-held, often erroneous, beliefs about the nature of human beings. For example, during the latter half of the Middle Ages, abnormal behaviour was predominantly thought to be the result of possession by devils or evil spirits. Often, "treatments" involved torturous, exorcistic procedures such as flogging, starving, immersion in hot water, etc., (Sue, Sue, & Sue, 1994, Chapter 1). In current times, however, the recognition of psychological disturbances (and biological dysfunction) has led to more humane treatment of the mentally ill within society (see also Rosenhan & Seligman, 1989) .

Most psychologists would agree that all aspects of functioning need to be considered in order to gain a fuller understanding of the human being. However, they will differ on what aspects they believe are of greatest importance. These differences reflect the variety of perspectives within psychology and the different lines of research being carried out by psychologists. These major perspectives are: *psychoanalytic, biological, developmental, humanistic, behaviourist, cognitive, and social* approaches to the study of human functioning. In practice, many psychologists do not adhere to just one perspective, but will take a somewhat eclectic approach.

Before considering the major perspectives in psychology, it should be noted that, historically speaking, psychology stems from a variety of strands. The two major influences come from philosophy and the biological sciences, which has led to different "schools" of psychology being developed. In this sense a "school" refers to a group of individuals who hold common notions about the nature of human beings. These influences are still with us today in psychology and are represented on any undergraduate degree in psychology, as well as having a significant influence on specialisms in psychology. For some good reviews on the history of psychology see, for example, Herganhan, 1992; Hothersall, 1990; Malim, Birch, and Wadeley, 1992; Watson and Evans, 1991.

PERSPECTIVES WITHIN PSYCHOLOGY

Psychology is ultimately the study of the person. Since there are many factors that work to "shape" each of us (e.g. genetics, learning processes, social influences, etc.), it is no surprise that psychology is a multi-disciplinary subject. Thus, when studying psychology at pre-degree and degree level, a number of perspectives or approaches are considered. For example, psychology can be looked at from a biological perspective, or from a combined approach (e.g. the study of psychological and social factors—a psychosocial approach). On the first year of a psychology course there is a wide coverage of the different perspectives and theories that have evolved within the discipline of psychology. The purpose of the rest of this chapter is to introduce the reader to the major perspectives encountered when studying psychology.

THE PSYCHOANALYTIC PERSPECTIVE

The psychoanalytic (also referred to as psychodynamic) approach is one of the oldest of the psychological perspectives. The onset of this approach can be traced as far back as 100 years ago when Sigmund Freud began his work. Indeed S. Freud (1856–1939) is often referred to as the "father" of the psychoanalytic approach. According to this view, human behaviour is governed by impulses that lie buried in the unconscious part of the psyche (a Greek word meaning "soul", currently used to refer to the "mind"). Freud believed that each of us experienced a series of psychosexual stages that would shape our adult personality. The behaviour we show to the world is like the tip of an iceberg, beneath which are the vast realms of the unconscious. Freud developed a number of techniques for studying the patients who came to him for treatment for a range of disorders (Atkinson, Atkinson, Smith, Bem, & Hoeksema, 1996; Herganhan, 1992).

Freud maintained that one's personality is made up of three parts—the *id*, the *ego*, and the *superego*. The *id* is thought to be the seat of all our basic, innate, drives and impulses such as sexual and aggressive drives. The id, for Freud, was the most inaccessible and primitive part of the personality, from which emanated such strong impulses that they could govern our overt behaviour. The second part of one's personality is the *ego*. According to Freud, this part of the personality acts to regulate the impulses emanating from the id and transforms them into a more socially acceptable form. The ego, therefore, acts to mediate between the drives of the id and the constraints of the outside world. The id operates on a "pleasure principle" because it seeks immediate gratification of the drives and impulses emanating from it. The ego operates on a "reality principle" because it transforms the basic drives of the id into a socially acceptable form. The final part of the personality is the *superego*. The superego develops within the first 5 years of life and, according to Freud, is the result of the child's incorporation of parental and social moral standards. The superego is seen as a "conscience mechanism", which works with the ego in order to mediate between the strong impulses of the id and to conform to what the external world expects of us. In this way, the personality is thought to be in a constant state of struggle as these individual components interact to deal with basic innate drives and outside forces. The system is said to be a dynamic one (see S. Freud, 1974).

In addition to the notion of a three-part personality, Freud believed that child development was a strong indicator of the type of personality characteristics a person would show as an adult. According to this aspect of Freudian theory, a person progresses through five basic stages in their psychosexual development, each of which brings with it a potentially significant change in the person's psychological makeup. (Psychosexual relates to psychological development that is strongly linked with sexual experiences.) The first three stages are experienced within the first 6 years of life; the final two occur between the age of 6 years and adulthood. A summary of these stages are: the *oral stage* (from birth to about 1 year); the *anal stage* (from 1 to 3 years of age); the *phallic stage* (with a major development between 5 and 6 years); the latency stage (from about 6 to 12 years of age); and the *genital stage* (from 12 years to adulthood). (For further discussion of these stages see Alloy, Acocella, & Bootzin, 1996; Gleitman, 1991; Sternberg, 1995.)

Freud maintained that if an individual progressed through these stages successfully then he or she would develop an adult personality that was, relatively speaking, problem-free (i.e. a person would not demonstrate maladaptive thought and behaviour patterns). However, if a particular stage was not "negotiated" successfully, then that person would develop what Freud referred to as a *fixation*. A fixation has been likened to having personality characteristics that are "frozen" in time, resulting in the manifestation of immature thinking and behaviour dependent on where the fixation lies. In some cases fixations can lead to various forms of neuroses (Alloy et al., 1996). So think carefully, if you are the type of person who is a chain-smoker, who likes chattering constantly, and/or who eats excessively, because according to Freudian theory, you might well be the victim of a fixation at the oral stage of your psychosexual development. (See also Atkinson et al., 1996; M.W. Eysenck, 1994.)

Freud's writings have undoubtedly had a significant influence on theory and application in the field of psychology, as well as on other fields such as psychiatry. A number of post-Freudian theories and techniques have emerged, many of which owe a great debt to Freud's work (see Atkinson et al., 1996; Gleitman, 1991; Hayes, 1994). Freudian theory is, like all theories, open to criticism (Fisher & Greenberg, 1977). For example, the theory has proved difficult to test under experimental conditions. Indeed, Freud's own writings offer little in the way of "hard data" that can be subjected to rigorous statistical analysis. There is little doubt that, in a time when discussion about sexuality was regarded as something of a taboo, Freud was unreserved in his explorations of the subject. Since Freud expounded his theory, many "post-Freudians" have written about the development of human personality, building on Freud's ideas and developing theories of their own. These include Carl Jung, Alfred Adler, and Karen Horney, to name but a few (see J.C. Brown, 1977; Fransella, 1981). In addition, a whole branch of psychoanalytic treatment has sprung up as a direct result of Freud's work. Freudian theory has also had an influence on the contemporary psychotherapies presently used in the clinical field (see Davison & Neale, 1994).

THE BIOLOGICAL PERSPECTIVE

Charles Darwin's *The Origin of Species* (1859) was heralded as one of the most significant influences on the way in which we viewed human nature. Prior to Darwin, thought was guided by the principle that human beings were unique in the sense that they were the only species that possessed a "soul". Therefore, humans were seen as being fundamentally different from other species. Darwin was a biologist who spent many years making comparisons between different species of animals (including humans). He suggested that humans had evolved out of other species, and should therefore be seen as part of the wider animal kingdom.

Darwin's work had a number of implications for the development of a biological perspective in psychology. M.W. Eysenck (1994) outlines four such implications. Each of these implications is briefly indicated here, along with an example of a current research focus that has directly influenced contemporary theory, research, and application. *First*, the notion that we should look at the interface between biological factors and psychological factors. An example of what influence this has had comes from the work currently being undertaken to discover the biological foundations of psychopathological disorders: for example, the current research into the potential causes of schizophrenia, as well as treatments that have been developed (see Rosenhan & Seligman, 1989; Sue et al., 1994). *Second*, the realisation that the study of animals can further our understanding of human functioning. For example, research into basic animal nervous systems, such as that of the Aplysia, has contributed to the development of a "model" of basic memory systems in humans (Pinel, 1996). *Third*, Darwin reinforced the view that heredity played an important role in the development of a particular species. Again, the genetic foundations of "normal" functions in humans, as well as in psychopathological conditions, are all too evident in contemporary psychology (see Hayes, 1994). *Fourth*, Darwin's observations on the variation between individual members of a given species and evolutionary selectivity has influenced our thinking on personality, intelligence, and individual differences in psychology. (See, for example, Atkinson et al., 1996; Sternberg, 1995.)

Currently, the biological perspective is an attempt to understand emotions, thoughts, and behaviour in terms of the physical processes taking place in the body (R.E. Smith, 1993). Biological psychologists have developed a good understanding of how our nervous system operates; the development of the brain and how its various sites govern different functions; and how artificial stimulants can impact on our physiology and, in turn, on our behaviour. Indeed, they have even begun to unravel the mysteries of the very building blocks of humankind—genetics. (See Atkinson et al., 1996; Carlson, 1994; M.W. Eysenck, 1994; Hayes, 1994; Kimble & Colman, 1994; Pinel, 1996; R.E. Smith, 1993.]

One example of the impact a biological approach has had on the study of humans comes from work on a biomedical model of abnormality. Abnormality is where a person is judged to be psychologically disturbed in terms of her or his personality and/or behaviour (Rosenhan & Seligman, 1989, Chapter 1). Normally, a clinical diagnosis of abnormality would only be made using a set of selected criteria and a range of diagnostic tools. The biomedical approach assumes that abnormality is an illness that exists within the body, as opposed, for example, to the idea that society is the cause of abnormality. This approach is founded on three basic assumptions. *First*, that the various manifestations of the abnormality—the symptoms—can be grouped together to form a syndrome. *Second*, that once the syndrome has been identified the physical aetiology or cause can be identified and located within the individual's body. *Third*, that a treatment, biological in nature, can be administered to alleviate the abnormality. (See Rosenhan & Seligman, 1989; Sue et al., 1994.) The biomedical approach has had a significant influence on theory and application with regard to conditions such as anxiety neurosis, depression, and schizophrenia (Davison & Neale, 1994; Sue et al., 1994).

Although the biomedical model has proved a useful framework from which many aspects of human functioning are studied, including abnormal behaviour, it does have its weaknesses. For example, psychological factors can lead to psychopathology, such as behavioural, cognitive, and, in some cases, early traumatic experience (Davison & Neale, 1994; Marks, 1969). Other approaches, such as the psychophysiological approach (the interface between psychology and physiological states) have proved useful as an explanation for a range of conditions, including everyday complaints such as migraine headaches (Sue et al., 1994).

DEVELOPMENTAL PSYCHOLOGY

Developmental psychology is defined as the scientific study of change in humans. Thus, within developmental psychology, a student will study how humans develop and why these changes occur. This approach encompasses changes that occur at the prenatal stage, right through to old age—with specific focus points. These focus points come at babyhood (from birth to age 3 years); early childhood (from 3 to 6 years of age); adolescence (from 6 to 12 years of age); young adulthood (from 12 to 18 years of age); middle adulthood (from about 18 to 40 years of age); mature adulthood (from age 40 to 65 years of age); and finally, the ageing adult (age 65 years onwards). Development through these stages is a gradual and continuous process, which means that a change from one stage to another may not be dramatic or even obvious (Kaplan, 1991).

Therefore, the focus of developmental psychology is change and this change can be quantitative or qualitative. So, what is the difference? A *quantitative* change in developmental psychology refers to an increase or decrease in some phenomenon, such as the average memory span of a child; changes in height; brain size, etc. An example of this is when one looks at the amount of words an individual learns to understand, which has a clear developmental trend. The average number of words an 18-month-old child can understand is about 20, with an increase in this to about 20,000 words at age 5, and through to about 80,000 words by the time she or he leaves school (Polermo & Molfese, 1972). Such an observation can be useful if we are developing learning strategies to increase the number of meaningful words above the average, but might not tell us why this change takes place. For that, perhaps, we would need to look for qualitative change. A *qualitative* change in developmental psychology, therefore, refers not merely to a change that is measuring a quantity (increase or decrease), but to a change in the structure or process of some phenomenon. An example of a qualitative change comes from the literature on the developmental aspects of cognition. For example, research supports the view that as they develop, children begin to use more strategies to aid remembering. When 5-year-olds are compared with, say, 12-year-olds, or adults, the youngest age group do not appear to utilise memory strategies, whereas the two older age groups do use strategies (see Kail, 1990). There are a number of explanations for this observation: for example, as the child develops she or he comes to learn the benefits of using memory strategies—a qualitative change. It is clear, therefore, that quantitative and qualitative observations can be used to understand the occurrences that take place at each of the stages in development outlined earlier.

The developmental perspective/approach represents a major area of theory and research in psychology and is usually well represented on any psychology degree course (as well as on pre-degree psychology courses). The topics covered in developmental psychology include: genetics; prenatal development and birth; the physical, cognitive, personality and social development at all the subsequent childhood stages (outlined earlier), as well as during adulthood. (See, for example, Atkinson et al., 1996; Gardner, 1982; Hughes & Noppe, 1985; Kail, 1990; Kaplan, 1991; Schroeder, 1992.)

One example of an area studied from a developmental perspective is that of the cognitive system and how it develops. Cognition refers to all those processes that allow us to encode and interpret sensory inputs from our world, and includes sensation, perception, imagery, memory, and thinking. One developmental theorist/researcher who has made perhaps the most significant contribution in this area is Jean Piaget (1896–1980). Piaget's theory is based on a lifetime's work in which he investigated a number of issues concerning cognitive development. Piagetian theory is a *stage* theory, one that envisages the cognitive system as developing through a series of stages, each representing a qualitative change in the cognitive structures of the child. The four basic stages are: the *sensorimotor stage* (from birth to 2 years); the *preoperational stage* (from 2 to 6 or 7 years); the *concrete operational stage* (from about 7 to 12 years); and the *formal operational stage* (from 12 years to adulthood). These stages can themselves be further divided into substages. (See, for example, Gardner, 1982; Hughes & Noppe, 1985; Kaplan, 1991 for details of stages and substages.) By the time the child reaches the formal operational stage, she or he is able to think through problems in their mind, before making a decision—indicating an advanced level of thinking.

Although Piaget's contributions continue to provide the impetus for much research in developmental psychology (see Best, 1995; Hughes & Noppe, 1985; Kaplan, 1991; Schroeder, 1992), his theory has been heavily criticised over the years; for example, in his failure to consider cultural differences in the development of strategies such as conservation, and his failure to identify important contextual cues that affect children's cognitive development and performance (see Donaldson, 1980; McShane, 1991 for a review of these criticisms).

As well as looking at normal growth and development, some developmental psychologists specialise in particular phenomena, such as those that are subsumed under the area known as developmental psychopathology. Developmental psychopathology refers to a branch of study that focuses on developmental disorders that manifest themselves at different stages of development. These disorders include childhood schizophrenia, autism, conduct disorders, and attentional deficit hyperactivity disorder; childhood anxiety; eating disorders; and mental retardation. (See, for example, Sue et al., 1994, Chapter 17; Van Hasselt & Hersen, 1994, Part IV; Wenar, 1994.)

HUMANISTIC PSYCHOLOGY

This approach or perspective began during the 1950s with the work of Carl Rogers and Abraham Maslow. The main tenet of this approach to studying humans is the idea that the person is constantly growing, changing, and attempting to reach their full potential. Humanistic psychologists focus upon self-direction, free will, and the ability of the person to make choices independently, as being the most important characteristics of the person. Humanistic psychologists believe, therefore, that we each have the potential to become a better human being and attain a higher level of functioning.

Abraham Maslow (1908–1970) is seen as the founder of humanistic psychology; that is, he developed it into a formal branch of psychology (Herganhan, 1992). Maslow is most widely cited for his theory of a "hierarchy of needs"—intrinsically linked with Maslow's belief that an individual strives to reach what he referred to as a state of *self-actualisation*. Self-actualisation basically refers to the idea that people attempt to fulfil themselves to their highest possible level of achievement in their personal life, work life, etc. However, Maslow believed few individuals ever reach self-actualisation. Maslow maintained that there were five basic classes of needs and that an individual strives to achieve the more basic class of needs before gradually ascending the hierarchy to reach her or his state of self-actualisation. The basic needs are similar to those striven for in the animal kingdom, whereas the higher classes of needs are thought to be distinct to humans (Atkinson et al., 1996).

Maslow's hierarchy of needs is represented in diagrammatic form in Fig. 1.1. At the lowest level, an individual strives to achieve her or his basic *physiological needs* such as food, water, oxygen, activity, and sleep. Once these needs have been satisfied, she or he can strive to achieve their next class of needs. The second class of needs relate to *safety*, which basically refers to having a secure and safe childhood, as well as security and safety as an adult. The third set of needs relate to the feeling that one *belongs* somewhere and is *loved* by others. Thus, having a good social life and good, stable relationships with others (sexual and non-sexual) would be primary aims at this stage of one's progression. The

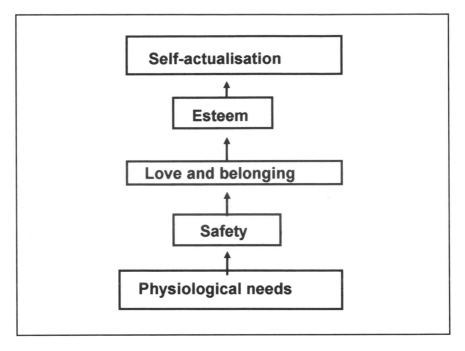

FIG. 1.1. Maslow's hierarchy of needs.

penultimate stage is *esteem*. This refers to the need to be respected by others, to be seen as honourable and as someone who makes a positive contribution to the well-being of others. If the individual reaches this level and fulfils her or his needs at this level, then she or he becomes *self-actualised*. Maslow's major contribution to psychology was the impetus he provided for the development of humanistic psychology itself (see Fransella, 1981; Hayes, 1994).

Carl Rogers (1902–1987) focused on the uniqueness of each person and how they viewed the world. Rogers believed that the role of an individual's self-perception and how they viewed the world would have a profound effect on their personality. For these reasons, Rogerian theory has become known as a "self" theory (Sternberg, 1995). Rogers believed that each of us has a self-concept and an ideal self. Self-concept refers to all those perceptions we have about ourselves, such as the way we look, or how good we are. The ideal self refers to those self-attributes each of us would like to posses. Rogerian theory further asserts that each of us struggles to match our actual self with our ideal self (a process very similar to Maslow's self-actualisation) and that by doing so we each have the potential to improve, grow, and change (Rogers, 1980).

One of the main contributions made by Rogers has been in his therapeutic technique called "person or client-centred" counselling. The basic aim of this form of therapy is for the individual to identify, with the help of the therapist, the differences between the actual self and the ideal self. This would involve the person's current status and some form of retrospective analysis, since the "self" develops from an early age and is affected by early experience. Where there is incongruous information (say, for example, the person overemphasises her or his negative points and underplays her or his positive points) then the therapist works to facilitate an acceptance of the negative points, as well as increasing the emphasis on the person's positive aspects. This form of therapy can be quite intensive, but is effective in improving the person's feelings of self-worth, self-esteem, and putting them on the path to "self-actualisation". (See, for example, Atkinson et al., 1996; Davison & Neale, 1994; Fransella, 1981; Hayes, 1994.)

Humanistic psychology is not without its critics. For example, it cannot be tested through the rigours of the scientific method, which must leave open the question of the validity of the approach. Also, if one looks throughout history, there are examples of people attempting to fulfil a higher class of needs without first securing a lower class of needs (as suggested by Maslow); for example, those who would starve themselves in order that others may be afforded their human rights, or those who would forfeit their own life for the good of society as a whole. In addition, as pointed out by a number of authors, Rogerian therapy (or other forms of so-called "insight" therapy) may not be appropriate for severe forms of psychological disorder (Davison & Neale, 1994). Since the pioneering work of Maslow and Rogers, humanistic psychology has continued to flourish; see, for example, the work of George Kelly (Herganhan, 1992).

THE BEHAVIOURIST PERSPECTIVE

The behaviourist approach, or behaviourism, became popular in the West about 80 years ago with the work of John B. Watson. However, as Hergenhan (1992) points out, the study of Objective Psychology (the psychological study of only those things that are directly measurable) was well developed in Russia before 1910. Before considering what contribution Watson, and others who came after him, made to the development of behaviourism, it is first necessary to consider the work of the Russian scientist, Ivan Petrovitch Pavlov (1849–1936).

Pavlov developed a theory that has become known as Pavlovian or classical conditioning. During the 1890s, whilst carrying out research into the digestive systems of dogs. Pavlov observed that, after a number of occasions, the dogs began to salivate as he entered the room prior to feeding them. Thus, the dogs appeared to have learned that his (Pavlov's) appearance signalled a subsequent event—the administration of food. Pavlov called this type of learning a conditional reflex because the reflex (e.g. salivation) is conditional upon learning from past events, in this case, that the presence of the experimenter signals the delivery of food. This response occurred when a contiguous association was formed between the presentation of food and some other event, such as Pavlov entering the laboratory and opening the food cupboard. Through a series of experiments, Pavlov gathered information and developed a theory now referred to as classical conditioning theory.

The basic principles of the theory are as follows: the subject is given an unconditioned stimulus (US)—such as food; the reflexive response is known as the unconditioned response (UR)—such as salivation; a second stimulus is introduced that would not normally elicit the UR, such as the sound of a bell, immediately followed by the presentation of the US (food). After several pairings of the bell and the food, Pavlov discovered that the mere sound of the bell alone was enough to elicit salivation. The result of this pairing is called the conditioned response (CR) since the bell had gained the power to elicit the response of salivation. The process by which the bell and food are paired is called reinforcement. The whole procedure is the basis of classical conditioning theory. Pavlov spent years expanding upon the various aspects of classical conditioning, such as extinction, generalisation, and discrimination (see Atkinson et al., 1996; Costello & Costello, 1992; Gray, 1979).

Intuitively, we are all familiar with the idea of classical conditioning: a hungry child, the ringing of a dinner bell, the child salivating at the thought of what comes next—dinner. Classical conditioning principles have been applied to a number of areas of research and application in the field of psychology; for example, to the study of conditioned fears and phobias; as a partial basis for interventions with offenders within the field of forensic psychology; as well as providing an explanation for a number of everyday occurrences. (See Blackburn, 1995; Quinn, 1995; Rosenhan & Seligman, 1989.)

J. B. Watson (1878–1958) believed that one could understand human functioning by adopting methods of enquiry that involved the observation of a person's behaviour and that this observation could be carried out by impartial, objective researchers. He also maintained that researchers could compare the results of their individual observations with a view to explaining the interaction between an external stimulus and a person's behaviour. Watson also believed that by understanding the conditions under which a particular behaviour, or set of behaviours, was performed, one could learn how to control behaviour (M.W. Eysenck, 1994). A strict behaviourist approach places little emphasis on mental processes being important in trying to understand humans and how they function within their world. Watson believed that all human behaviour could be broken down into basic components, and that these could be found in terms of learned stimulus–response (S-R) associations which were built up over time by the two events (stimulus–response) being repeated (Hayes, 1994). So for Watson, the aim of the psychologist was to develop a full understanding of how learning via S-R associations took place, and how this could be applied; e.g. how behaviour could be changed. He further asserted that it was sufficient to explain behaviour as the result of S-R associations repeatedly occurring in the environment, a limitation that has led some theorists to extend this further—most notably B.F. Skinner.

B.F. Skinner (1904–1990) is often credited with taking Watson's ideas further. Like Watson, Skinner emphasised the role of stimulus–response associations as a way of explaining human function and placed little emphasis on mental processes within the individual's mind. Skinner's major contribution was the introduction of the concept of *operant conditioning*. Based on the work of E.L. Thorndike (1874–1949), operant conditioning extended the S-R theory and emphasised the importance of reward following a particular behaviour. Skinner proposed that *reinforcers*, some *operant*, and a *discriminative stimulus*, were crucial to understanding the interaction between an environmental stimulus and response behaviour. A *reinforcer* is some event that impacts upon the probability of some behaviour occurring. If the reinforcer is positive then its presence increases the probability of repetition of a behaviour or event that preceded it. If the reinforcer is negative, its removal increases the probability of a recurrence of an event that preceded it. Punishment is different because its presence decreases the probability of recurrence of a behaviour or event that preceded the punishing stimulus. An *operant* refers to the event itself that is affected by the positive or negative reinforcement, or punishment. The *discriminative stimulus* refers to a "signal" that signifies that a particular reinforcement is likely to occur if the operant reveals itself (e.g. a particular behaviour).

The major difference between classical and operant conditioning lies in the nature of the response to a given stimulus. Whereas classical conditioning offers a good explanation of behaviour that is simple, reflexive, and automatic in nature (such as the knee-jerk response, the eye-blink response, and autonomic responses), operant conditioning, by contrast, focuses on behaviour that is voluntary in nature—an example of which would be behaviour that is carried out for a reward. (See

Atkinson et al., 1996; Hayes, 1994; Hergenhan, 1992). As with classical conditioning, S-R theory has acted as a good framework from which a number of specialisms in psychology explain maladaptive human functioning, as well as offering an explanation for everyday phenomena. Some examples include the study of psychopathological disorders (such as learned fears and phobias); a partial basis for interventions in the field of forensic psychology and forensic psychiatry; and contributions to more contemporary theories such as social learning theory—which itself offers good insights into many social phenomena, such as the study of aggression, prejudice, and so on (see Aronson, 1994; Baron & Byrne, 1994; Blackburn, 1995; Faulk, 1994; Rosenhan & Seligman, 1989). In addition to these applications, operant conditioning theory has led to a whole field of study in relation to *behaviour shaping*—which basically refers to the gradual changing of an organism's behaviour through the process of applying the principles of operant conditioning theory. Behaviour shaping (also known as behaviour modification or successive approximation) has been successfully applied in a number of fields, not least within a clinical context (see the work on behaviour therapy in Davison & Neale, 1994, Chapter 19; and Alloy et al., 1996, Chapter 19).

One drawback with a traditional behaviourist approach to the study of humans is that it does not place enough emphasis on the role of other factors in determining a person's actions, such as the cognitive processes that can lead to a given behaviour. Another reason why people sometimes resist behaviourist explanations is that it (behaviourism) is seen as reducing human functioning to merely animal responses, likening the human species to other animals—which possibly reduces the human qualities each of us like to feel we have. Having said that, current behaviourists accept that cognition does play some role in mediating behaviour, although they would argue that its role is of minimal importance.

THE COGNITIVE PERSPECTIVE

The cognitive perspective has grown enormously since the pioneering work of Donald Broadbent during the 1950s, and emphasises the role of processes associated with the mind in human functioning. Cognitive psychologists are interested in the ways in which a person's memory is organised and operates, how an individual acquires language skills, her or his problem-solving abilities, how a person forms images about the world, how belief systems are formed, and what impact such factors have on behaviour, as well as artificial intelligence (see, for example, Atkinson et al., 1996; Baddeley, 1990; M.W. Eysenck & Keane, 1995). In addition to this, some cognitive psychologists attempt to gain an understanding of the cognitive system by observing and testing people who have suffered brain damage that has led to specific cognitive deficits, an approach referred to as cognitive neuropsychology (see Ellis & Young, 1994; McCarthy & Warrington, 1990).

Two key aspects provided the impetus for establishing a cognitive psychological approach as a mainstream psychological perspective. First, behaviourism was on the decline during the 1950s as more emphasis was placed on the role of a person's thought processes in determining behaviour. Second, scientists were developing computers which, it was believed, could simulate the way in which humans think. It was within such an era that Donald Broadbent conducted research into how, under particular circumstances, humans were able to actively gather information from their environment and interact with that information to solve particular problems (Broadbent, 1958). In short, Broadbent believed that each human being was an active information processor. This concept has developed into a keystone of cognitive psychology and the contributions made by Broadbent have given rise to a mass of theoretical thinking and empirical research (see, for example, Baddeley, 1990; Best, 1995; M.W. Eysenck & Keane, 1995). Cognitive psychology currently represents one of the biggest areas of theory, research, and application within the field of psychology, and accounts for a sizable portion of the psychology section of most university libraries (see also M.W. Eysenck, 1994; French & Colman, 1995; for good introductory coverage of cognitive psychology).

As with other approaches, cognitive psychology has also proved fruitful in combination with other perspectives, with some current psychologists adopting a combined approach—particularly in the applied field. One example of this is the *cognitive–behavioural* approach, which has been applied to the study of a number of aspects of human functioning. This approach basically focuses on the interface between cognitive factors and behaviour, and has led to the development of a number of cognitive–behavioural therapies for a range of conditions. For example, cognitive–behavioural therapy for mood disorders such as depression focuses on "faulty" cognitions or thoughts and how such cognitions can contribute to psychological and behavioural symptoms associated with a given mood disorder (Sue et al., 1994). The process here is to identify negative cognitions, such as "I am a bad person, the problems I face are insurmountable"; compare these thoughts with the reality, such as "you are not really a bad person, the problems faced can be overcome"; and change or re-structure the overall cognitive pattern with more adaptive thinking. An example might be for the individual to emphasise the good points about her or himself, or try to be more realistic about the situation she or he is in. When used in a structured, elaborated way, such an approach can be effective for treating conditions like depression (for example, see the work of Aaron T. Beck, 1967, 1983), and often appears most effective in combination with other forms of treatment such as behavioural methods, drug therapy, etc. (Sue et al., 1994), as well as proving applicable for a range of other conditions (see Rosenhan & Seligman, 1989).

The cognitive perspective has also been criticised. For example, one early criticism of cognitive psychology was its heavy reliance on a laboratory-based approach to studying cognition. Inevitably, when testing phenomena in a laboratory setting—where a high degree of control can be achieved—the findings are said to lose their external validity; i.e. their relevance to real-life situations. These days, cognitive researchers carry out laboratory and field-based studies, and even combine the two—as is the case with quasi-experimental approaches (M.W. Eysenck, 1994). Of course, the major limitation with taking too strict a cognitive perspective is that the human being cannot be understood just by exploring their thought processes (although these are important). This is why cognitive psychology is often combined with other perspectives to provide a multi-dimensional approach to studying humans (see also Sternberg, 1996).

SOCIAL PSYCHOLOGY

Since we all live and function within a social world, it is not surprising that many theorists and researchers have studied what effects the social environment has upon the thoughts, emotions, and behaviour of the individual. Although there are some exceptions, humans actually like contact with others. Social psychology is the study of what effects groups have on individuals, and how being a part of a group or, in a wider sense, a society, affects a person's thinking, feelings, and behaviour. Social psychology has emerged as a major focus of study both from an experimental and a non-experimental approach, as well as offering viable explanations about real-world phenomena (see e.g. Aronson, 1994; Baron & Byrne, 1994; Myers, 1993). Some of the major topics covered in social psychology include the study of social influence—which covers conformity, obedience, and compliance (Baron & Byrne, 1994, Chapter 8); social cognition (Myers, 1993, Chapter 5); group dynamics—such as polarisation, leadership, and decision-making processes (Sabini, 1992, Chapter 3); attitude formation and attitude change (Sears, Peplau, & Taylor, 1991, Chapters 5 & 6); and aggression (Aronson, 1994, Chapter 6).

Let us take one example from this, and provide some insights into theoretical and research developments within the field—that being the work produced on the phenomenon generally known as "aggression". Aggression is usually defined in terms of an "intentional infliction of some form of harm on others" (Baron & Byrne, 1994). Violence can be seen as a deliberate act to inflict physical harm on some other person. There is a vast literature on the nature and origins of aggression, ranging from an "ethological approach" (see the work of Konrad Lorenz, 1966); to a "motivational approach" (see the work of J. Dollard and colleagues; Dollard, Doob, Miller, & Sears, 1939); to a "psychoanalytic approach" (see the work of S. Freud). All these approaches provide interesting insights into aggression, but they falter when it comes to explaining questions such as, "What role might society play in mediating aggression?" Social psychology offers a different, and arguably more viable, explanation of factors that might mediate aggression.

Social learning theory (Bandura, 1977) has been applied to the study of aggression and includes the work on "social modelling", which suggests that aggression can be learned via an individual (quite often a child) observing aggressive behaviour in another person, who is called a social model and who might in this case be a parent. Thus, a child might copy aggressive and violent behaviour from observing such behaviour in other people. Indeed, increased levels of aggressive and violent behaviour have been seen to occur in an experimental setting where children were exposed to aggressive "models" (Bandura, 1973; Bandura, Ross, & Ross, 1961, 1963). Such findings have offered useful insights into some of the potential causes of aggression and have had an impact on wider issues such as the relationship between viewing violence on television and film, and elevated levels of overt aggression. Indeed, some researchers have suggested that violent viewing does, in fact, lead to increased and long-term manifestations of violent behaviour (Eron, 1982; Leyens, Camino, Parke, & Berkowitz, 1975). However, it should be noted that other researchers have discovered mixed findings on the effects of television viewing on aggression (see, for example, Freedman, 1984). It has also been noted that other psychological factors, such as cognition, also play a role in determining aggressive behaviour (Berkowitz, 1993).

In addition to the development of social psychology as a major perspective within psychology, applied social psychology has also recently developed. Applied social psychology is the application of theoretical and research aspects of social psychology to everyday, real-life phenomena (Baron & Byrne, 1994). Applied social psychologists study a number of topics, but away from the traditional laboratory-based studies that dominated psychology before the mid-seventies.

These topics include: social behaviour and environmental factors, such as the work carried out on "personal space" and the effects of crowding; the study of health-related behaviour, such as the social dynamics involved in doctor–patient interactions; social psychological factors and ill-health; and work within a legal forum, such as eyewitness testimony, courtroom dynamics, and jury size—all of which represent current, active areas of research within applied social psychology (see Baron & Byrne, 1994; Sabini, 1992; Saks & Krupat, 1988; Sears et al., 1991).

FINALLY

It should be clear from this introduction that psychology is a multi-dimensional subject, drawing from a number of perspectives. This is inevitable given the wide range of forces that impact on the individual and is also reflected in the specialisms studied at postgraduate level in psychology. For good introductory texts on the main perspectives within psychology see, for example, Atkinson et al., 1996; M.W. Eysenck, 1994; Gleitman, 1991; Hayes, 1994; or Sternberg, 1995. In addition to understanding relevant theory and research findings in psychological literature, *you* will be expected to develop the knowledge and skills needed to carry out research yourself. You will be given tutoring in this. The research component is reflected in several parts throughout the remainder of this book.

CHAPTER TWO

A study guide to lectures, seminars, and tutorials

INTRODUCTION

As a student, your contact time—the amount of time you are required to attend formal academic sessions—will be made up mainly by your attendance at lectures, seminars and, in some cases, tutorials. The only exception to this is the time spent in practical-related classes.

PRACTICAL CLASSES

For research methods courses on a psychology degree, particularly where the degree is a Bachelor of Science (BSc), practical classes can make up a substantial component of such courses. In practical classes you are taken through procedures for conducting literature searches, designing and running studies, analysing the data from those studies, and producing a final report on the research. The aims of a research methods course are to enable you to learn the basic skills involved in carrying out research: to familiarise you with the different approaches to research and with relevant statistical analyses and other methods of measurement; to help you to develop report-writing skills; and to provide you with hands-on experience of running experiments and using appropriate laboratory equipment, as well as relevant computer packages.

Typically, for practical classes, your contact time will include a lecture component, a laboratory class component, and in many institutes, a related seminar/tutorial class. The lecture component will provide you with the necessary theory and empirical knowledge; the practical class component will provide you with the practical experience of researching; and the seminar component can be used to provide a forum for discussions related to your whole experience of research methods. The exact organisation of practical classes will vary from institute to institute, and it is therefore difficult to provide guidelines on how best to prepare for such sessions. At the beginning of each research methods course, you should be provided with a timetable for the lectures, practical classes, and (where appropriate) seminars. In addition to this, you should be given ongoing advice about exactly what preparation you need to do for each of these sessions. For example, if you were at the "design" stage of research you might be given a lecture on designing experiments, experience in designing an experiment in class, and be asked to come along to the seminar to discuss different types of designs (having first been directed to reading sources). It might be a good idea to ask the research methods tutor at the beginning of the course to explain the exact interrelationship between the different components of the methods course.

The aim of the remainder of this section is to provide guidelines on how best to prepare for and study during lectures, seminars, and tutorials.

CONTACT TIME GENERALLY

Local Education Authorities often require that you attend at least 80% of all course contact sessions (lectures, tutorials, seminars, etc.). Those students who do not meet this requirement run the risk of having their funding withdrawn. The amount of contact time will vary from institute to institute, but a contact time of between 10 and 14 hours or so each week can be expected. You are expected to engage in self-directed study in addition to this. In general, the amount of class time is reduced as you progress through the course. Thus, at the final-year stage it is highly likely that you will be working independently, outside formal contact sessions, for much more of the time than would, say, a first-year student. There are a number of reasons for this: for example, the research methods classes are replaced by your undertaking a self-directed (but supervised) psychology project or dissertation in the final year of an undergraduate degree (which is seen by many as the pinnacle of the degree course). The rest of your contact time is likely to be spent attending lectures, seminars, and tutorials. So, what do these sessions involve?

Before going on to look at what these sessions involve and how best to prepare for them, it might be useful to consider two approaches to learning that can be used in such sessions. Over the years these different approaches to learning have been referred to as the *having* or *being* mode of study, or as *passive* and *active* learning, and, more recently, as *deep* and *surface* processing (Barnes, 1992; Fromm, 1979; Smith & Brown, 1995). These approaches can play a crucial role in learning during contact sessions on a degree, as well as for any preparatory work a student does for examinations, etc.

Different approaches to learning

In 1979, Eric Fromm distinguished between those students who were in a having mode of study and those who were in a being mode of study. The *having* mode is used to describe those who merely obtain a body of knowledge through a relatively passive mode of study: the lecturer imparts a body of knowledge on a subject, the student listens, takes notes, and reproduces part of that body of knowledge for some future event (e.g. an exam). The *being* mode of study refers to where the student becomes actively involved in the material being presented, thinking through the material, making notes of relevant points from the material presented, and posing questions that allows her or him to develop an understanding of the concepts and issues involved in the topic, as well as its relation to other subject matter—for example, how the research/theory compares with other research findings and/or theory in the literature. The mere accumulation of knowledge will not by itself stimulate thought processes, whereas an active participation in the material itself will enable the perceiver to critically assess, analyse, and draw conclusions from that material.

Active learning, then, is a skill that should be developed throughout a course of study (for example, in lectures, seminars, and tutorials) and should be used when carrying out coursework, as well as revision for examinations. When preparing for coursework in the form of essays (see Chapter 3) and practical reports (see Chapter 4), organising the literature in relation to the task can facilitate active processing (i.e. organise the literature around a particular question/topic in an essay, or around the aims of the research project). Also, when revising for examinations (see Chapter 5), organising information taken from the literature can provide a powerful cue for recall. Active study is also about a student using the information in such a way so that she or he analyses the information, thinks critically about the information, develops and/or links ideas together from various sources, and presents a critical account of the information in relation to the particular topic, issue, or question being addressed. This is quite different from a *passive* approach to learning, where a student merely collects information and regurgitates it at some future event (e.g. an exam). A student who develops active learning skills will benefit from this in terms of their ability to organise, remember, and use information picked up on the course, and through their own literature searching.

Current research has shown that using different approaches to learning does lead to different outcomes (B. Smith & Brown, 1995). Specifically, it has been found that using a *deep* approach to learning has a more beneficial effect than using a *surface* approach. These different approaches can be summarised as follows (see B. Smith & Brown, 1995).

A deep approach involves:

1. Focusing on what you think the main argument(s) are in an author's piece of work (or what is required by the tutor setting your work).
2. Drawing relationships and distinguishing between new ideas and previous literature.
3. Drawing relationships and distinguishing between evidence and argument.
4. Relating the evidence to everyday life.
5. Organising and structuring the content of a piece of work.

A surface approach involves:

1. Focusing purely on the discrete components of the text (e.g. describe a phenomenon; recall facts).
2. Memorising and regurgitating information.
3. Forming associations between concepts and facts without reflection.
4. Failing to draw relationships between, or distinguish between, new or previous evidence and argument.
5. Seeing the task as an imposition placed upon you by some external agency (i.e. your tutor).

The more adept you become at using an active or deep approach to learning, the more you will come to understand the material you are reading and writing about, and the more of that material you will remember. Also, by using such an approach, your marks and final degree classification can be improved (see e.g. Ramsden, 1988). The first year of an undergraduate degree course can be the ideal time for you to acquire and develop these learning skills. Such skills should be utilised, as much as possible, in all your contact sessions (lectures, seminars, tutorials) as well as in on-course assessments.

LECTURES

During a lecture, you will be presented with a range of materials (for example, lecture notes, slides, diagrams, etc.) and you are responsible for taking concise, easily understood notes that you can elaborate on at a later date. Some lecturers provide handouts containing the main points about the lecture topic, and, in some cases, a full set of references cited for that lecture. Be sure to ask where the references can be found if you have not been given the full reference source by your tutor (e.g. are they from a particular book or a particular journal article?). Most lectures will be a 1-hour affair, but sometimes you may be asked to attend a 2- or even 3-hour lecture (in which case there is normally a break half-way through the lecture). It is normally left up to the student's own conscience whether to attend a particular lecture. However, if the attendance at a lecture is consistently low, the lecturer may decide to take a formal register.

Lectures are seen as a very important part of the psychology course because it is here that you are presented with a framework of the phenomena studied on that particular part of the course. During this time, relevant theory and research is presented in a concise and coherent form. Some lecturers will actively encourage students to ask questions, whereas others will ask you to refrain from asking questions during the lecture, but will be willing to answer any questions at the end of the lecture, or in a related tutorial session. Although lectures may seem like a very one-sided affair (lecturer talking: student listening) students can enthuse a lecturer by appearing interested, alert, and attentive. However, do bear in mind that not all lectures will be fascinating. Very often, what you get out of a lecture depends on not just how it is presented, but how much you enjoy the particular topic under consideration and your own preparation. So, how can one study effectively during lectures? And what behaviours should be avoided? What follows is a list of activities likely to occur (on the part of the student) during a lecture, and brief comments as to their likely effectiveness as a learning strategy.

Copying down lecture notes from the overhead projector or from what is said by the lecturer

This is often seen as a passive strategy because, although you are getting the information down, you are probably not thinking a great deal about that information.

A much more effective strategy would be to re-write the information into a form that has more meaning to you, perhaps accompanying each paragraph with a question or two (which you can either use as a basis for questioning the lecturer afterwards, contemplate yourself at a later date, or discuss with fellow students after the lecture).

Asking the lecturer questions about the topic being considered in the lecture

This is a very useful and active strategy because when asking questions you become alert and are actively thinking about the subject.

Although a recommended strategy, asking questions during a lecture might be discouraged by some lecturers. Perhaps it would be best to wait until after the lecture has finished. After all, if everybody in a lecture hall containing 100 students wanted to ask questions, there would be little time left to complete the lecture itself!

Answering the questions posed by the lecturer

This is seen as an active process because again it requires you to think critically about the topic.

Remember, you are not expected to know all the answers, so even if you find that your answer is not quite accurate, do not be put off answering questions.

Writing down your own ideas and thoughts on the subject

This is a very active strategy and is highly recommended during lectures. It will help you to distinguish between lectures and may make a particular lecture more memorable (i.e. it can help with what is known as the consolidation process in memory).

Asking yourself relevant questions

Ask yourself the following questions about the material:

How does that part of the literature compare with other parts covered?

How can the literature be organised or structured?

What is worth noting and what is not?

What are the major issues or topics of controversy?

Are there problems/limitations with the information presented?

(See e.g. Barnes, 1992).

Remember, the main aim of a lecture is to provide you with a framework of the topic under consideration, from which to work. This means that you must spend some time outside the lecture on fleshing out your lecture notes. As you progress through your course, particularly at degree level, you will be expected to search for information such as textbooks—which are called secondary sources—and journal articles—which are called primary sources—that fall outside those to which the lecturer has referred you. You must do this by reading around the literature the lecturer has referred to in the lectures, and summarising relevant theory and research before adding this to your own set of notes. If you do this as an ongoing task you will find that it makes revision much more manageable, rather than leaving it all until nearer the deadline for the assessment or examination. For further advice on studying in lectures, see, for example, Marshall and Rowland, 1993; Saunders, 1994.

SEMINARS

A seminar can take one of a number of forms. It can be where you as a student are expected to prepare and present some piece of work to the rest of the seminar group. Or, alternatively, it can be where a group discussion ensues about particular phenomena (e.g. a theory, piece of research, etc.), and students are encouraged to provide their own informed opinions about the topic under discussion. The precise format the seminar takes will be determined by the course tutor. A seminar group will usually consist of the lecturer and several students. The number of students in a seminar group can vary, depending on the numbers enrolled on a particular course and the nature of that course. A seminar group will normally consist of the same group of people throughout the whole year and each one typically lasts for about 45 to 50 minutes. The lecturer will provide the initial briefing, during which you should be fully informed about what is expected of you in terms of your preparation and the amount of time for which you should aim to speak during the seminar itself. For example, you may be asked to read a chapter from a book, or a journal article, and prepare and present a summary of that piece of work to the seminar group. You will also be expected to handle some questions from the group about the material you have prepared, so make sure you prepare well for such a session.

Quite often there will be ground rules laid down about whether or not you can use visual or audio equipment in support of your presentation, such as slides, or acetates on an overhead projector. Again, your tutor should fully brief the group as to the guidelines and/or ground rules at the beginning of the course. Normally, there will be a number of presenters (i.e. students), each of whom present a summary of a piece of work, the aim of which is to address one part of a topic or question under consideration. Once these presenters have finished a group discussion follows, with the lecturer there to guide the seminar through its various stages. If you are at all worried about an impending seminar presentation, or you are not sure how to organise your presentation, the tutor should be willing to meet with you beforehand and provide some guidance.

PREPARING FOR THE SEMINAR

As stated earlier, your tutor will provide you with a full briefing sheet and/or explain to you what you are required to do for the seminar. The briefing (written or oral) should (ideally) tell you what question or topic is to be addressed in the seminar; what your contribution is expected to be; which piece of work you are expected to consult and summarise; and for how long you are expected to talk. Advice on actually preparing for the seminar can be provided by the tutor on request.

Once you know what the topic is and you know what material you need to access, start preparing sooner rather than later by collecting the information from books and journal articles well in advance of the seminar. Read the material and make brief notes about the main points of the information, always trying to relate it to the question set in the seminar briefing (or topic to be addressed). DO NOT prepare exhaustive notes that amount to a re-write of the whole material: this is not what the seminar is about and will not look good on the day. Your fellow students and the tutor will not appreciate your sitting there reading several notebooks on the topic!

If you feel happier, and the facilities are available to you, use some visual aid such as an overhead projector, but make sure the notes you place on the acetates are brief and contain the salient points only (assuming that your tutor agrees to this). Many people like using visual aids because they take the attention away from them (the presenter) and onto the projected image, therefore reducing the anxiety of having several people watching their every move. If you do use transparencies, make sure they are clear and that you do not put too much information onto one transparency. Also, make sure they are legible. Using handouts is also a good way of diverting attention and can actually help the other students by allowing them to think about the subject rather than hurrying to take down notes about what the presenter is saying. Handouts also provide permanent reminders of the information discussed in seminars. Remember, it is possible that the material you cover in seminars will be part of the final examination—you might wish to check this point with your tutor.

Perhaps the most daunting part of the seminar process is when you are asked questions on the topic, either from your tutor or your fellow students. Most students, of course, will not be looking to ask too difficult a question—after all, they will have to take their turn as presenter! If you are asked a question, take your time, think for a moment, perhaps repeat the question (it gives you more thinking time), and try to make some informed answer. Remember, psychology is ultimately to do with human experiences, so even if you forget all the grand theories, you should be able to come up with something from your own past experience (but this is not as good as providing an informed answer based on the literature). If you really haven't a clue what the answer might be, admit it and ask if others might make a contribution.

In some institutes, attendance at seminars will be monitored by the tutor taking a register, in others it may not. In most cases you will be asked to present perhaps only once or twice throughout the particular course (or module), such as an Introduction to Psychology course in your first year—but you are expected to *attend* all seminar sessions. In some institutes seminar presentations are marked and contribute to your overall assessment on a particular course.

WHY BOTHER WITH SEMINARS?

Presenting to small groups is a very useful skill to develop, not just because it is part of your learning experience, but because it has a great deal of relevance to other aspects of your life. So what are the uses of seminar presentations?

Presenting at conference.   Some of you (for example, in your final year of study) may go on to present your work at a conference. Indeed, there are a number of undergraduate conferences that take place each year to which you could be invited to present a summary of your final- year project/dissertation. Presenting your work at a conference will enable you to gain respect in your particular field and have your work published in conference proceedings. Conferences are good places to impress other people in your field, so if you want to be taken seriously in psychology, present at conferences. It also looks good on the curriculum vitae (cv).

Improves your social skills.   Developing the skill of presenting to small groups can help to overcome the nerves many people experience when discussing things with a group of individuals who are familiar with the topic. The more you learn to control those nerves in a group discussion setting, the easier it becomes.

It can be good practice for job interviews.   Presenting at a seminar can be very good practice for performing at a job interview. The interview is somewhat like a seminar in that you will be asked questions about material you have prepared (i.e. your cv or application form) by a number of people. You will be expected to present a concise and coherent argument as to why you are best suited for the job. The more practised you are at seminar presentation, the better you will come across at interviews.

Some don'ts in relation to seminars
1.   Don't panic! most academic institutes will have an adviser who can provide guidance on how to control panic.
2.   Don't leave the preparation for a seminar until the last minute.
3.   Don't rush things; take the time needed to get the information across clearly in the seminar.
4.   Don't just miss the seminar. This will not only annoy your tutor, but will cause problems for the rest of the seminar group (and you'll probably be asked to present another one in its place).

It would be wrong to try and make out here that seminars are easy to do. They can (as indeed tutorials can) be a somewhat daunting experience. However, nobody is out to make the student look a fool, or induce any unnecessary angst, so do not act as though you were going before a firing squad. Prepare well, accept that you don't know all the answers, and deal with the situation. Seminars can play a very important part in the learning process (if they are organised correctly), and they do get easier with practice.

TUTORIALS

A tutorial is typically an event where either a small group of students and the lecturer get together, or sometimes a single student meets the lecturer on a one-to-one basis. The main aim of a tutorial is to offer the student the opportunity to follow up material covered in the related lecture course and to ask the lecturer questions relating to that material. A tutorial can provide the student with the ideal opportunity to ask the lecturer to clarify theory, research, or general points about the topic under consideration, rather than trying to pin the lecturer down outside formal contact time. Where you have a very busy lecturer, such as a professor who spends a lot of her or his time preparing for publications, or attending conferences or busy meetings, a tutorial may be the *only* chance for you to question her or him at any length.

So the tutorial differs from the lecture in that you are not just one of a large lecture audience listening to the lecturer expounding views on a particular topic, nor is it like a seminar where you are expected to prepare and present some piece of work. But you are expected to come to a tutorial prepared to question and to make active, spoken contributions (the same expectation applies to the lecturer). With ever-increasing numbers of students in further and higher education, tutorials can tend to get a little large in their numbers, in some cases becoming rather like small lecture groups. However, most lecturers consciously try to avoid this and will therefore run a number of tutorial groups in order to keep each one to a manageable size.

Another problem arising from the large numbers might be a situation where a part-time lecturer is hired to take some of the extra tutorial (or seminar) load away from the course tutor. When this happens it can sometimes be a little off-putting for students having to question one lecturer about material presented by another lecturer. If this happens, do not be put off; the lecturer who takes the tutorial, or seminar, should be familiar with the area or be fully briefed by the main lecturer running the course and presenting the lectures. One major problem students have with tutorials (and with seminars) is their feeling that, because they are not experts in the field, they are afraid of looking stupid in front of the lecturer and other students if they get the information wrong, or have to admit that there is something they are not sure about. Tutors are fully aware of this and know that even the brightest of students sometimes find it very difficult to master new material (after all, your tutor will have had to learn the material in a similar way!). So do not be put off asking questions you think are relevant, or offering what you think are useful contributions to the tutorial (or seminar). In fact, your fellow students will probably be silently thanking you for asking a question that they were too afraid to ask!

SOME FINAL POINTS ABOUT SEMINARS AND TUTORIALS

In some institutes of Higher Education, seminar and tutorial work is marked and may contribute towards your final grade, whereas in others it is not marked—a point that is worth checking with the relevant course tutor. It is felt that attending and contributing to seminars and tutorials will help you develop learning skills that cannot be acquired in the traditional lecture setting, and will therefore help you to improve your performance in your coursework (and examinations). Taken together, seminars and tutorials will help you to:

1. Clarify ideas and literature that you have not understood.
2. Evaluate material by looking at different viewpoints.
3. Summarise material (e.g. a journal article) into a manageable form.
4. Relate the information you (and your fellow students) have read to the specific question/topic under consideration.
5. Express yourself clearly and coherently when taking part in discussions.
6. Discuss related topics not necessarily covered in lectures, such as applied aspects or everyday aspects of the phenomena.

Developing these skills can help enormously on the course. *In particular they can help you to develop the type of critical thinking necessary to become an active learner and promote deep processing.* If you are able to develop such skills, you should find that your coursework—be it an evaluative essay, a critical appraisal of a piece of research, or your performance in a final examination—should all benefit from this. Developing and enhancing these skills in the first year of study can have a positive effect on the two subsequent years that typically make up the bulk of an undergraduate degree in psychology; and remember, in most institutes it is years 2 and 3 that determine your final degree classification. These skills are not only crucial for studying for your degree, but will also help in your personal development. So, make the most of your contact time. For further reading on preparing for and studying during seminars and tutorials, see, for example, Barnes, 1992; Marshall and Rowland, 1993; Saunders, 1994.

CHAPTER THREE

A guide to essay writing and referencing

INTRODUCTION

Essay writing is a skill that an undergraduate student needs throughout the whole of a psychology course. In fact, in most institutes of Further and Higher Education, essays can make up the bulk of a student's coursework; so taking the time to get it right is time well spent. The composition of an essay can take any one of a number of forms, depending on what key phrase or phrases are contained in its title. Some key phrases likely to appear in essay titles are provided further on in the chapter. The size of essays on undergraduate courses vary, but usually the word length increases from about 1200 to 1500 words in the first year of a course, to about 2000 to 2500 words in the second year, and up to around 3000 to 3500 words in the final year. An example of a good coursework essay can be found in Appendix 1 towards the end of the book, and should be read in conjunction with the information provided here. (The essay represents a 1500-word, first-year piece of coursework graded as a first-class piece of work. The mark assigned to the essay was 75%.)

What follow, then, are guidelines on the main stages of essay writing and on writing style within an essay, and a guide to referencing in psychology. The guidelines on writing style were provided by, and reproduced here with the permission of, Neil McLaughlin Cook, who is Head of Psychology at Liverpool Hope University College. The guidelines on referencing were provided by, and reproduced here (with some modifications) with the permission of, Sue Thomas and Keith Morgan, both of whom are Lecturers in Psychology at Liverpool Hope University College.

STAGES IN ESSAY WRITING

A good essay, particularly one focusing on an academic subject, is rarely completed in one great sweep. General study skills advice suggests that the craft of essay writing needs to be learned over time, and that one good way of learning about the process is to break it down into clearly identifiable stages (see Northedge, 1990). The following are therefore brief notes on the stages involved in writing an essay.

Giving some thought to the title
This sounds obvious, but it is a fact that some students rush headlong into an essay without giving enough thought to what is required for that essay: the title can tell you what is required. (See the major keywords included later in this chapter.) One useful strategy might be to jot down, in one or two sentences, what you think the title means. For example, is it a request for a descriptive essay, where you are required to provide a detailed account of the topic under consideration? Or are you required to write an argumentative type of essay, where a particular point of view is stated and the writer attempts to defend (or disprove, if appropriate) that viewpoint by looking at the evidence on balance? For further consideration on the differences between descriptive and argumentative essays, see M. Smith and Smith, 1990.

Carrying out a literature search
Before attempting to write the essay, you must first gather together the relevant information and organise that information in some way. Fortunately, most tutors will provide some supporting references when setting essay questions (or may provide starter references), so you need to access these sources. In addition, you could carry out a computer search in the library using specific keywords that are in the essay title. If you do carry out a computer search, make sure you have combinations of keywords to hand, so that you can be more specific in the search process (otherwise you might end up with hundreds of citations from the computer!).

If you already have notes from relevant lectures, organise these by perhaps rewriting the relevant parts of the lecture notes in relation to the specific topic covered in the essay title. For example, if your essay title was: "Discuss how effective behavioural therapy is as a treatment or intervention for anxiety disorders", then you need to look through your lecture notes for Abnormal Psychology and pick out those most relevant to the essay topic. Make additional notes from the extra sources you have accessed and add these to the extracted lecture notes. Finally, add to these any relevant supporting references (e.g. Seligman, 1992) and organise under sub-headings (for example, definition of phenomena; supporting evidence; counter arguments). Carrying out a fairly thorough literature search is a very important part of preparation for essay writing and should not be done superficially. For further reading on searching the literature, see Barnes, 1992; Marshall and Rowland, 1993; Saunders, 1994.

Devising an essay plan

Once you have thought about the title and organised your notes you might decide to draw up a plan of the essay. This will entail your putting down on paper a series of ideas, suggesting how the essay will flow from the introduction, on to the main body of the essay, and through to the conclusion stage. Be prepared to change these ideas or scrap what you have written and start again (e.g. if, on a second look at the plan, you feel it is not the best way to organise the information). However, research has found that using an essay plan, or even several essay plans, does not lead to higher marks for the essay itself (Norton, 1990). Having said this, an essay plan can be of some use in providing a structure around which to organise the essay.

EXAMPLE OF AN ESSAY PLAN

The following simple essay plan could be used to organise an essay on "Discuss how effective behavioural therapy is as a treatment for anxiety disorders":

Please note: The final version of your own essay should not be subsectioned using the first three headings that follow; but it should always contain a Reference section at the end. You do not, however, need to supply a Reference section at the end of formal examination answers.

1. *Introduction:* Definitions of keywords; explaining what is meant by the question set (if appropriate); briefly suggest how the essay will attempt to address the question/topic.

2. *Main body of essay:* Definition of "clinical" anxiety; examples of anxiety disorders; what types of treatment are available; relevant theory underpinning treatment(s); the efficacy of the treatment(s); supporting references; criticisms/limitations of treatment(s).
3. *Concluding section:* Overall conclusion(s); overall comments which directly address essay question/topic in the light of previous literature cited.
4. *Reference section:* Citation of primary and secondary sources (see final section of this chapter for further details on referencing).

Writing a first draft of the essay

Once you reach this stage in the process you are just about ready to begin writing the essay itself. The first draft does not have to be one great sweep from introduction to conclusion(s); it can develop in parts. You might write part of the introduction section on one page, move on to describing the concepts under study on another page, and so on. This stage is aimed at getting down on paper, in a basic essay form, the information you have collected in note form. You should write the draft in a fluent and convincing manner, as if you were trying to persuade the reader that your views are the most valid. Once you have begun writing, try to carry on and finish the draft: stopping and pondering over every few sentences will throw you off track and interrupt the flow of ideas you should be experiencing (you will still refer to your notes for supporting theory and research). You need to give your full attention to this draft, as though you were thinking through a talk you were giving to an attentive audience.

Correcting the first draft

Once you have written the first draft, you should read through the essay, analyse its structure and content, and make the necessary changes. You should check that the essay:

1. Has a coherent structure.
2. Flows from one part to the next (are there link sentences between paragraphs? does one paragraph follow logically from the previous paragraph?).
3. Has enough support for your arguments (i.e. references).
4. Has enough up-to-date literature (as well as historical literature).
5. Shows evaluation of relevant theory/research.
6. Has *fully addressed what was set out in the title* (e.g. have you answered the question posed in the title?).
7. Has reached some conclusion(s) about the topic.
8. Incorporates a complete Reference section.

Final modifications

When you finally reach this stage, what may be needed is no more than a re-write of the essay, incorporating the changes proposed at the previous stage. If you can, try to get some independent source to provide critical feedback, such as another student. You can always reciprocate by reading a draft of her or his essay. Don't spend any more time on this than you must. If you feel you have done the job properly, submit it and move on to the next task.

SOME IMPORTANT POINTS ABOUT COURSEWORK ESSAYS

Norton's (1990) research on the relationship between strategies used by students to write essays and tutors' strategies for marking has produced some findings relevant to this section. In addition to her finding that essay plans do not lead to higher marks, she also found that those essays providing relevant support in the form of citations of theory and research (which, in the first year of a degree, are often derived from books) produced higher marks. Whilst the majority of students thought that providing good content and structure were the main things to aim for in an essay, rather than putting forward an argument based on the literature addressed, tutors' marks indicated that it was those essays that *produced an argument on the basis of research evidence* (which can be derived from secondary sources, i.e. books) that achieved high marks. Structure and content do feature in marking, but not nearly as highly as argument, critical analysis, and so on. Norton concludes, amongst other things, that students should:

1.   Be clear about what the tutor who is marking the script is looking for in the essay.
2.   Concentrate on presenting their essay in the form of an argument, rather than relying on factual or descriptive accounts.
3.   Support their arguments with research-based literature.
4.   Spend several hours (six or more) preparing and writing the essay.
5.   Discuss their mark with the tutor in order to gain feedback.

By developing these strategies further, the student can improve her or his essay writing skills enormously, and should, of course, achieve better marks.

A GUIDE TO WRITING STYLE

Neil McLaughlin Cook

Several stylistic conventions apply to academic writing in Psychology. This guide outlines four such conventions, which you should try to follow in your essays; it concludes with a warning about the consequences of substantially deviating from two of them!

1. Using appropriate terminology

When writing essays, you are expected to choose your words carefully, and you should try to avoid phrases that are imprecise, ambiguous, or imply irrelevant value judgements.

- An example of an *imprecise* phrase commonly found in students' essays is: "Psychologists argue that...". A more appropriate phrase might have been: "Several psychologists (e.g. Bryant & Bradley, 1985; Cashdan & Wright, 1990) argue that...". Similarly, your tutor will expect you to use precise technical terms (such as "mean", "median", or "mode"), instead of relying on more general terms used by the person in the street (such as "average").
- An example of an *ambiguous* phrase is "man's achievements", where "man" is intended to refer to human beings of both sexes, but might be interpreted as referring to males only. A better essay would use a less ambiguous phrase like "human achievements".
- An example of a phrase that implies an *irrelevant value judgement* is "man and wife". A better essay would use parallel terms such as "husband and wife", or "wife and husband".

Note that two of the problems shown above were eliminated by using non-sexist language. The British Psychological Society (1990) has published a very helpful set of guidelines for using non-sexist language, which also considers how to avoid ethnically biased language. This document is well worth consulting and contains much practical advice that will help you to ensure that your writing meets the three criteria outlined here.

2. Infrequent use of the first person

New students often use the first person ("I" or "we") in their essays. However, this is rarely appropriate in formal academic writing in psychology, and you should seek to adopt a more impersonal style. (An exception to the "avoid the first person" rule might be when discussing your own personal experiences. Note, though, that arguments in psychology essays should normally be based on published theories and research, with personal experience being used at the most as supplementary information.)

Shown below are two reasons why students use the first person, together with an indication of alternative ways of achieving the same goals.

Signalling

One reason for using the first person is to signal the structure of an essay (e.g. "We will now discuss Freud's theory of personality..."). Certainly, there is evidence that including signals in the text can be a sensible strategy. For example, Spyridakis and Standal (1987) have shown that signals can have a positive effect on reading comprehension, and so it is reasonable to infer that they might help a tutor to understand your essays! However, it is possible to incorporate signals into an essay without using intrusive phrases like "We will now discuss ...". For example, here are some phrases that signal a move to another section of an essay:

Another important theory of personality was developed by Freud ...

Therefore, laboratory experiments imply a negative answer to the question. However, a different picture has emerged from the results of field studies ...

Indicating that an idea is your own

A second common reason for using the first person is to indicate that an idea is the student's own (e.g. "I think Blogg's experiment is invalid because ..."). Certainly, tutors' marking criteria often imply that it can be fruitful to include your own ideas in an essay. For example, at Liverpool Hope, the criteria for first-class honours include "clear evidence of originality ..." Fortunately, originality can be indicated without using the first person in academic writing. You are expected to cite your source for all the ideas you include in your essay, and so your tutor will assume that any idea for which no source is cited is your own! Therefore, although the first extract following implies that an argument has been obtained from a student's reading, the second implies that the argument is the student's own:

McKay (1996) argues that these findings are ambiguous because ...

These findings are ambiguous because ...

3. Expressing ideas in your own words

When marking your essays, your tutor will want to know if you understand the material you are writing about. Indeed, Norton (1990) found that "understanding" was judged by tutors to be one of the most important criteria they used when marking essays. One good way to demonstrate understanding is to *express ideas in your own words*. If, instead, you write an essay that consists merely of extracts copied or paraphrased from books, you are giving your tutor no information about whether you understand the material. For example, take the sentence: "Wherever Gestalts intervene, they do not do so as autochthonous factors, but as assimilatory schemata" (adapted from Piaget & lnhelder, 1973, pp. 402-403). It is an easy matter to copy the sentence, or paraphrase it to "Wherever Gestalts intervene, they do so as assimilatory schemata, not as autochthonous factors", without trying to understand any of the technical terms! Therefore, you should try to write your essays, as far as you can, in your own words. (If you feel that you do have to include an extract from a published source, then also include an accompanying comment to demonstrate that you have a good understanding of it! For example, one explanation of the quote might read: when subjects perceive an unusual figure as having characteristics of a regular shape, this is not the result of an innate tendency to perceive stimuli that have regular features, but instead the subject's use of previously encountered shapes as a framework to guide their perception of new figures.)

When asked to write essays in their own words, students sometimes raise the following objections.

Textbooks express ideas so much better than I can

This may be true (but don't underestimate your own writing abilities). However, your tutor wants to assess *your* work, not Glassman's (1995) work! Nevertheless, you may occasionally feel that the force of the author's point would be lost unless the point was quoted verbatim. In this case, you should cite the full source of the quote, including page number(s), as follows:

Watson (1980) argued that the experiments outranked most others "when it comes to cruelty, deception, ingenuity and sheer absurdity" (p.23).

I don't deliberately keep to the wording in a text: I base my essays on my notes, and forget which notes were copied verbatim

This reveals a need to improve your skills in notetaking from texts. Try making notes mainly in your own words rather than in complete sentences; where your notes do follow the same wording as a text, try writing your essay in different words, rather than merely copying your notes.

4. Organising ideas in your own way

It can be tempting to let your essay follow the ready-made structure in a book. However, simply to copy someone else's structure gives no indication that you have understood what you have to do, and will probably result in a structure which does not meet the demands of the question set: the only way to show your tutor that you understand the demands of the question is to organise the material yourself. Such a strategy may well reap rewards in terms of marks, because Norton (1990) found that "answering the question" was judged by tutors to be the single most important criterion when marking an essay!

Finally: what happens if a student's essay *does* keep closely to the wording and structure of the student's sources?

Nobody will bother about the odd phrase being the same as a phrase in a book. However, if a large part of the essay appears to stick too closely to your sources, your tutor will notice it and take action. If the material taken from your sources is properly acknowledged as such, your tutor might simply comment that it would be preferable to rely more heavily on your own words.

However, if a large proportion of your essay consists of copied or paraphrased extracts from sources you do not properly acknowledge, this will be regarded as *plagiarism*, which means presenting other people's work as your own. Plagiarism could involve copying material from other students' essays as well as copying material from books and, in all Universities, it is treated very seriously, no matter what source the material has been taken from. The detailed procedures for dealing with plagiarism will vary across institutions, and the penalty imposed in any individual case would depend on the extent of the plagiarism and the circumstances involved. Typically, though, the penalties available to the examiners might range from a reduction in the marks awarded for an essay to a recommendation that the student not be allowed to graduate! The simple rule in relation to plagiarism is: don't risk it!

Some keywords to look out for in essay titles

What follows are some keywords typically used by tutors when setting essay questions, and what these terms mean.

> *Account for:* Reason why something is as it appears.
> *Analyse:* Examine (in detail) the components of something.

Assess: Estimate what value can be attached to something (this definition can also be used for the term *Evaluate*).
Comment: Make remarks/explanatory notes on something.
Compare: Estimate the similarity of one thing to another.
Contrast: Estimate the differences between two or more things.
Consider: Weigh up the merits of something (or deliberate).
Define: Provide some meaning of.
Describe: Provide details of something.
Discuss: Examine by argument.
Distinguish: Differentiate between two or more things.
Evaluate: Judge the importance of in the light of criteria.
Examine: Investigate the phenomenon in detail.
Explain: Clarify some phenomenon(a).
Illustrate: Provide detailed analysis to make a point clear.
Interpret: Explain the meaning of something.
Justify: Provide support for an argument or action.
Outline: Detail the most essential aspect(s) of something.
Relate: Make some connection between things.
Summarise: Provide an account of the main points.

A GUIDE TO REFERENCING

Sue Thomas and Keith Morgan

The term referencing means the citation of sources of information referred to by the essayist (or experimental researcher). Referencing is a method of providing your reader with the evidence and/or sources that you have used to support your arguments or statements etc., in a piece of written work. Referencing enables the reader to find the original evidence so they can check your interpretation or read further.

Referencing falls into two parts:

1. *CITING* the source *in the text*.
2. Giving full information *in the REFERENCE section* on how to find the source.

A reference section is NOT the same as a bibliography. A reference section must include EVERY source *cited* by you in the text, and NOTHING ELSE. A bibliography is just a list of the sources you consulted while preparing your piece of work, whether you *cited* them or not. *In psychology you have to give only a reference section.*

There are several referencing systems in use. *In psychology you must use the HARVARD system.* (Since the American Psychological Association [APA] uses the same system, you may find this referencing system referred to as either APA or Harvard.) When you have your psychology degree it will be assumed that you can freely communicate with all the other qualified psychologists. Using a common referencing system is part of our shared language. Other subjects use different systems, but you must use the Harvard (APA) system for all your psychology assignments. Because this is so important, some psychology departments (or sections) penalise students for poor referencing *which means that you may lose marks for poor referencing.* Check what the policy is in your own psychology department/section. If you follow this guide you should not have any problem with referencing correctly: it may be laborious, but it's not hard.

The two most common types of sources referred to in psychology are books (in part or in whole) and journal articles. This section provides a brief guide to the acknowledgment of reference sources both within the text of, and at the end of, an essay or practical. If you have thoroughly searched through the whole document without finding what you need, then you should ask a psychology lecturer (preferably the tutor who will mark your piece of work) for assistance. Check you have read this guide carefully first! One of the features of academic writing, and one that distinguishes it from more informal styles (e.g. when writing a newspaper article) is that you are expected to indicate fully your source for all the material mentioned throughout your work.

CITING SOURCES IN TEXT

Using the Harvard (APA) system means that every time a reference to a particular source is made, the author's surname and year of publication are given. If the author's surname appears naturally in the sentence, the year is given in brackets; if not, both surname and date are given in brackets. For example:

Freud (1936) was mistaken in thinking …
This was considered to be correct at the time (Freud, 1936)

If you have given the date in the text, you don't have to repeat it in the brackets:

In 1936, a summary of the yearly conference (Freud) …

Common sense dictates that in the rare circumstances that *both* the name and the date are clear in a well-written sentence, then a citation in brackets can be omitted:

1936 was also the year in which Freud published his summary of the yearly conference.

But if you are in any doubt, *cite.*

If you have cited more than one source by the same author from the same year (anywhere in the whole piece of work), these are distinguished by adding lower-case letters (e.g. a,b,c, etc.) after the year, within the brackets:

Baddeley expounded his theory on memory (1983a) ...

Baddeley reinforced the notion of the applicability of his theory (1983b) ...

If there are two authors, the surnames of *both* should be given before the date every time the source is referred to:

It will now be understood how it is that the psychotherapeutic procedure we have ... (Freud & Breuer, 1955).

If there are more than two authors then the first time the source is referred to *all* the authors must be given, but subsequent citations can be referred to by the first surname followed by "et al.":

(1st time): A nominal scale measures just the property of difference and nothing else (Elmes, Kantowitz, & Roediger, 1995).
(2nd time): A nominal number does not assist in measuring a person's attributes ... (Elmes et al., 1995).

When referring to more than one author with the same surname it is necessary to include the initial each time it is cited:

... this importance of the id in childhood is of great significance (S. Freud, 1936).
The importance of the id in childhood has been overstated (A. Freud, 1936).

When giving multiple citations they must appear in alphabetical order:

Psychology has often been likened to a "science of the mind" (Gleitman, 1991; Sternberg, 1995).

More than one citation of the same author should be given in chronological order:

Beck (1967, 1983) showed that ...

DIRECT QUOTATIONS

Direct quotations must include the following: the author's name, date, and page number. Short quotations should be presented within quotation marks as part of the text (*Example 1*), longer quotations should be indented (*Example 2*).

Example 1:
Personal Construct Theory has questioned the validity of Freudian or behaviourist theories; for example: "In the theory of personal constructs the person is not segmented into 'learning', 'cognition', 'motivation', 'emotion' ..." (Fransella, 1981, p.147).

Example 2:
Thus, Fay Fransella (1981) claims that:

> In the theory of personal constructs the person is not segmented into "learning", "cognition", "motivation", "emotion" ... (p.147)

which is typical of the Construct Theory approach.

Omissions from a quotation (as at the end of the two examples above, where the quotation ends before the sentence in the original) are indicated by an ellipsis (three dots). Words added to the quotation by you to improve the sense are enclosed in square brackets:

Alvin Stardust (1974) has claimed hegemony over youth groups with soundbites such as: "I [Stardust] am the leader of the gang ..."(p.1), which echoes the rhetoric of Glitter (1972).

NOTE: YOU WILL SAVE YOURSELF A GREAT DEAL OF TIME AND EFFORT IF YOU KEEP A RECORD OF ALL YOUR REFERENCES AS YOU MAKE NOTES, READ, ETC.

PRESENTATION OF A REFERENCE SECTION

Your Reference section must come at the end. Always give it a clear heading. The format of references included here is dependent on whether you have consulted a *primary* source or a *secondary* source. So what is the difference?

A *primary* source basically means that you have read the original, whole, text (e.g. an article in a journal, a chapter in an edited book contributed by the author, a book by the author, etc.), which you have found and consulted. A *secondary* source refers to where you have found an original piece of work mentioned, discussed, or described (e.g. text-books are usually full of citations of articles and books), so the textbook is a secondary source for these papers, etc. Note that almost every academic piece of work will cite other items, as can be seen from the Reference sections.

It is important that you give the reference for the source you have actually used (i.e. if you read about Sigmund Freud's work in Atkinson et al., then you should reference Freud in such a way that the reader knows that you have read about his work only in a textbook, rather than in the original). For example, if you are writing an essay on Freudian theory and you go to your departmental library and find Freud's book *Totem and taboo*, which you take notes from and cite in your essay, then in the Reference section you would give a straightforward reference to that book:

Freud, S. (1912). *Totem and taboo*. London: Routledge & Kegan Paul.

However, if you had read about *Totem and taboo* elsewhere, such as in another text or book (as in the example used here), then you would list the secondary source in the reference list, and refer to the primary source in the text citation; for example:

Text citation: Freud's (1912) book *Totem and taboo* (as cited in Strachey, 1958).

Reference list: Freud, S. (1912). Totem and taboo. In J. Strachey (Ed.), *The standard edition of the complete psychological works of Sigmund Freud (1958) Vol. XIII*. London: Hogarth Press.

Different types of sources (e.g. books, journals, edited collections) are presented in slightly different ways in your Reference section. Information on each of these methods is given below. Remember, your Reference section should be organised so that the references appear in alphabetical order by first author. If the same author appears on more than one occasion, then the order of referencing for that author is by date of publication of work. If one author has produced several pieces of work in the same year, indicate this by alphabetical suffices (a,b,c, etc).

For example:
Baddeley, A.D. (1983a). Working memory. *Philosophical Transactions of the Royal Society of London, Series B, 89,* 708–729.

Baddeley, A.D. (1983b). *Your memory: A user's guide.* Harmondsworth: Penguin.

Listing a reference for a book
For books, each entry should give certain basic information as follows:

1. Author's surname followed by initials as given on the title page of the book (not from the spine or cover of the book). As this is the vital reference for location of work in a library make doubly sure that the name is correctly spelled. If the writer edited a collection rather than wrote the book indicate this by placing (Ed.) after their name; (Eds.) if more than one editor.
2. The year of publication in brackets. This is usually shown on the back of the title page of the book you have consulted.
3. The full title of the book, including any subtitle. Use a capital letter for the first word of the title and the subtitle, and for any proper nouns. This should be underlined or in italics if word processed. If it is a revised edition or a second/third/etc. edition, follow the full title with (Rev. ed.) or (2nd ed.) or (3rd ed.) etc., as appropriate. If you have cited a new edition, remember to give the date of the edition you used. Reprints, impressions, etc., are not important because they do not involve any changes in the text.
4. The place of publication (if more than one is shown on the title page of the book, check the reverse of the title page, which will usually give details of which office actually published this volume) and name of the publisher (the place and the name are separated by a colon [:]). It is not necessary to add details such as "Limited" or "& Sons" etc.

For example:
Becker, H.S. (1966). *Social problems: A modern approach.* New York: Wiley.
Paivio, A. (1979). *Imagery and verbal processes.* Hillsdale, NJ: Lawrence Erlbaum Associates.
Paivio, A. (1983). *Imagery and verbal processes* (2nd ed.). Hillsdale, NJ: Lawrence Erlbaum Associates.

Listing a chapter from an edited book
The chapter is described first, followed by a description of the book it is taken from:

1. Chapter author's surname, followed by initial(s).
2. Date of chapter, in brackets. (Usually this is the same as the book, but not always, as for example, where there are collections of material which has been previously published.)
3. Title of the chapter in full.
4. The word "In" followed by the initial(s) and surname(s) of each of the editors of the book from which the chapter comes, and the abbreviation (Ed.) or (Eds.) in brackets, followed by a comma.
5. The year of publication of the collected volume, if different from the date of the chapter.
6. The full title of the book, including any subtitle, using a capital letter for the first word of the title, the subtitle, and any proper nouns. This should be underlined or italicised. Give edition if appropriate.
7. The place of publication (if more than one is shown on the title page of the book, check the reverse of the title page, which will usually give details of which office actually published this volume) and the name of the publisher (the place and the name are separated by a colon (:)). It is not necessary to add details such as "Limited", "Inc.", or "& Sons".

For example:
Hobfoll, S.E., Banerjee, P., & Britton, P. (1994). Stress resistance resources and health: A conceptual analysis. In S. Maes, H. Leventhal, & M. Johnston (Eds.), *International review of health psychology: Vol. 3.* Chichester: Wiley.
Reyna, V.F. (1985). Figure and fantasy in children's language. In M. Pressley & C.J. Brainerd (Eds.), *Cognitive learning and memory in children: Progress in cognitive development research.* New York: Springer-Verlag.
Rogers, C. (1990). Motivation in the primary years. In C. Rogers & P. Kutnick (Eds.), *The social psychology of the primary school.* London: Routledge.

Listing an article from a journal
For an article from a journal, adhere to the following format:

1. Author(s) surname(s) and initial(s).
2. Date (in brackets).

3. Title of paper (initial capital letter only).
4. Full name of journal (this should be underlined or italicised). It is better if you write the title of the journal in full: do not use standard abbreviations.
5. Volume number, in *italics* (part number, if relevant).
6. Page numbers (first to last).

For example:
Norton, L.S. (1990). Essay-writing: What really counts? *Higher Education, 20,* 411–442.
Roediger, H.L. (1980). Memory metaphors in cognitive psychology. *Memory and Cognition, 8,* 231–246.
Hitch, G.J., Halliday, M.S., Schaafstal, A.M., & Heffernan, T.M. (1991). Speech, "inner speech", and the development of short-term memory: Effects of picture-labeling on recall. *Journal of Experimental Child Psychology, 51,* 220–234.

If you cannot obtain part of the information needed to write a full reference, then give what details you know and indicate that the omission is deliberate. The most common element missing is the date: it is convention to use the letters "nd" to show this.

For example:
Squid, G.Y. (nd) The ethnography of adultery in royal clans. *Monarchy and Monarchs, 13,* 32–48.

Listing general media
Weekly and monthly (and some other) publications (often called "periodicals") may number each issue from page 1 (instead of carrying on from the page number that the previous issue finished at); if so, it is very useful to give the exact date of the issue. For example, the exact date for a weekly *New Scientist* will be something like (1993, December 4) (the date will be given after the author as usual); for the monthly *Scientific American* the exact date might be (1993, December).

For example:
Horgan, J. (1994, July). Can science explain consciousness? *Scientific American, 271,* 72–78.
Kingman, S. (1994, September 17). Quality control for medicine. *New Scientist, 143,* 22–26.

References to articles from magazines, newspapers, etc., can often use the same structure as scientific papers.

For example:
Highfield, R. (1994, January 19). Great brains fight for your mind. *Daily Telegraph,* 14.

References to sources like television programmes, radios, videos, audio-cassettes, and newspapers/magazines/etc., for which you don't have enough information to use the above styles, should be written so as to give all the help that you can in tracing the source.

For example:
Equinox. (1992). *Born to be gay?* Channel 4, 21 February.

Listing tests and other materials

Questionnaires, scales, stimuli, etc., all need to be referenced. This is easy: you simply treat them as books, chapters, journal articles. If the scale comes from a chapter, reference as a chapter. Test manuals are regarded as books for this purpose.

For example:
Dickman, S.J. (1990). Functional and dysfunctional impulsivity: Personality and cognitive correlates. *Journal of Personality and Social Psychology, 58,* 95–102.
Eysenck, H.J., & Eysenck, S.B.G. (1969). *Personality structure and measurement.* London: Routledge.

CHAPTER FOUR

A guide to research methods & empirical research report writing

INTRODUCTION

Since psychology is ultimately about the scientific study of behaviour, it is necessary to consider what methodological tools are used in order to gain a fuller understanding of that behaviour. These different methods of investigation should be seen in terms of each one serving a particular purpose, rather than in terms of one method being "better" or "worse" than another. M. Eysenck (1996) likens it to a golfer selecting a particular golf club for a particular type of shot: it is simply a matter of selecting the one that is best designed for that purpose, not because one club is "better" than the other. This chapter is in three parts. Part 1 introduces the reader to research methods in psychology. Part 2 highlights the major ethical considerations in research. Part 3 provides guidelines on empirical research report writing. An example of a completed report can be found in Appendix 2 and should be consulted in conjunction with the information here.

PART 1   RESEARCH METHODS

On a Bachelor of Science (BSc) psychology degree course (as well as on many other types of psychology course), research methods, and associated analysis, comprise a large component of the course, culminating, on most degree courses, in a large-scale final-year research project. The rest of this section is taken up with introducing the reader to the fundamentals of literature searching, hypothesis/question formation, research methods, and associated analysis. Having a knowledge of research methods and analysis serves a number of functions:

- It enables you to assess the value of findings reported in various sources, such as newspapers, formal reports, magazines, etc.
- It enables you, as a researcher, to assess the value of existing lines of research (such as, for example, the long-term efficacy of a particular drug treatment).
- It provides the motivation for new research projects, which can be aimed at furthering our knowledge of relevant theory/research.

It should be noted that a student who is new to psychology is not expected to develop a full grasp of all the techniques outlined here, but will be introduced to many (but not necessarily all) of these concepts and procedures within their first 2 years of study on a BSc psychology degree course.

THE QUANTITATIVE/QUALITATIVE DISTINCTION

Social scientists in general, and psychologists in particular, make a distinction between *quantitative* and *qualitative* research. *Quantitative* research involves the collection of numerical data in order to answer questions about some phenomenon (for example, the use of questionnaires to estimate how many people use alcohol or other substances, or the administration of cognitive tests to estimate how well people remember under certain conditions, and so on). Statistics are applied to the data in order to summarise the findings and enable the researcher to draw inferences about the wider population from which the sample is drawn. *Qualitative* research is best suited for situations where the phenomenon under study does not lend itself easily to quantitative methodologies (such as attempting to find out why a person uses addictive drugs, why people commit crime, and so on). In reality, many researchers combine both approaches. For example, a "qualitative" researcher may collect some data in order to bolster her or his argument; and a "quantitative" researcher may first ask series of general questions in order to guide hypothesis formation, before going on to test these hypotheses using a quantitative methodology. Whatever approach is used, a researcher will normally carry out a literature search in order to provide some basis for the study.

LITERATURE SEARCHING

Searching and evaluating the literature available on a particular phenomenon provides the best source of ideas that can guide a research project. It also enables the researcher to discover what research others have carried out in the area and what they have found. Ultimately, the scientific approach is about testing some formal hypothesis (or set of hypotheses). What is a hypothesis? The term hypothesis refers to an operational definition about the exact comparison that makes up the aim of the study (Bausell, 1986). In this sense it enables the reader to focus on exactly what the study is about—which is to provide some answer to a research question or to test a particular prediction. All research, regardless of whether it is "quantitative" or "qualitative", should be guided by some overall hypothesis(es) or research question(s) that needs to be addressed. Before reaching the stage of hypothesis formation, or the development of overall research questions, the researcher must first come up with a source for the idea. Research is not developed in a vacuum.

The source can be some common-sense notion of what one expects to happen—what we believe to be true or false. Relying on pure common-sense notions to guide research can be problematic; they could be wrong. An idea could come from our observations of the world around us. Observations of personal experiences and social events can provide a hypothesis that merits testing (Cozby, 1989). However, on a degree course it is likely that you will be expected to consult a formal body of literature (books and published articles) based on established theory and research. Established theory and research can be used to generate ideas for further research and as a basis for a particular research project. Theories can provide the impetus for research. A theory is a formal set of statements that summarise and explain a particular phenomenon— for example, a theory of memory. A theory can act as a guide to how we can make sense of what we observe in our world and it can generate new knowledge about real-world phenomena. Theory can also be modified by what is discovered through research.

A formal literature search can begin with the references provided on course—that is, by the course tutor for a particular topic (e.g. a course reference list on, say, abnormal psychology). Good reference sources in the form of books provide useful lists of relevant primary and secondary source material in their reference sections. As a student progresses through the psychology course, she or he should become less dependent on a standard set of references provided by the tutor, and become more familiar with library searching. This is particularly true for the final-year dissertation/research project. Library searches can provide a wealth of critical information with regard to what research has already been carried out in the area of interest and can come in a number of forms. Some of the major sources of library searching are outlined below.

Journals

Journals are collections of work, both theoretical and research-based, which are published at regular intervals (e.g. some are published on a monthly basis, some on a quarterly basis). These are sometimes referred to as periodicals. In these journals, theorists expound their latest views on some phenomenon (for example, a theory of personality) and researchers will publish their latest findings. The majority of these journals are "peer-reviewed"—which means they have been scrutinised by other researchers in the field and have been judged as worthy of publication for the wider research population. These journals are usually listed in a library catalogue under specific headings, depending on the nature of the articles they contain. The major listings include the following:

General psychology. Subsumed under this area are journals that include literature reviews, theory, and other general topics within psychology. See, for example, the *Psychological Bulletin*, and the *Psychological Review.*

Clinical and counselling psychology. These journals contain articles pertaining to clinical and counselling psychology (e.g. mood disorders, schizophrenia, anxiety neurosis, addiction, behaviour therapy, counselling theory and application, and so on). See, for example, the *Journal of Abnormal Psychology*; the *Journal of Counselling Psychology*; the *British Journal of Psychiatry,* and the *Journal of Clinical Psychology.*

Experimental journals in psychology. These journals contain experimental articles on a range of psychological phenomena (e.g. memory and cognition, perception, animal and human behaviour, genetics, learning and motivation, cognitive science, psychophysics, neuroscience, and so on). See, for example, the *Journal of Experimental Psychology* (including the subdivisions of *General*; *Human Learning and Memory*; *Perception and Performance*; and *Animal Behaviour Processes*); *Memory and Cognition*; the *Journal of Verbal Learning and Verbal Behaviour*; *Cognition*; *Perception*; and the *Quarterly Journal of Experimental Psychology* (Parts A and B).

Developmental psychology. Subsumed under this heading are journals that contain articles on a range of developmental issues. These include: child development, experimental investigations into child psychology, infant behaviour and cognition, gerontology, applied areas of developmental psychology, and so on. See, for example, *Developmental Psychology*; the *Journal of Experimental Child Psychology*; *Child Development*; and *The Gerontologist*.

Personality and social psychology. These journals contain articles on research into personality and social psychological phenomena as separate topics, but also combinations of the two, as well as applied research in these fields. See, for example, the *Journal of Personality*; the *Journal of Personality and Social Psychology*; the *Personality and Social Psychology Bulletin*; and the *Journal of Applied Social Psychology*.

Applied psychology research. These journals contain articles on a range of applied areas of psychology, such as educational psychology, applied behaviour analysis, applied cognitive psychology, occupational psychology, environmental psychology, criminological psychology, and so on. See, for example, the *Journal of Applied Psychology*; the *Journal of Educational Psychology*; the *Journal of Applied Behaviour Analysis*; and *Occupational Psychology*.

See Cozby (1989) for further listings of journals in these areas.

Psychological abstracts

Psychological Abstracts is a source that lists the abstracts from the major psychology journals in a non-evaluative way (i.e. without judging the content of the article). This can prove to be a very fruitful way of searching a large literature source, but provides you with only a summary of the piece of literature in the form of an abstract, and its source. These days, this source is available on computer format and is referred to generally as *PsycLit*. *PsycLit* is accessible in most university libraries, within which a librarian should be able to advise you how to operate this system.

It should be noted that in the first year of a degree course, a student is not expected to have a full grasp of literature-searching techniques, but will be expected to learn more and more about such techniques as they progress through their course—with the help of their tutors (see e.g. Breakwell, Hammond, & Fife-Shaw, 1995; Cozby, 1989; Elmes, Kantowitz, & Roediger, 1995; Robson, 1994 for further information on searching the literature.) Once the researcher has conducted a literature search and decided what research hypothesis(es) or research question(s) they wish to address, then they need to decide *who* they will study and *what method* of study will be used. The first part of this relates to sampling procedures and the second part relates to the type of methodology adopted by the researcher—both of which are considered here.

SAMPLING PROCEDURES

Sampling refers to the selection of a group of participants (selected for the study) from a wider population. Since no researcher is likely to have access to all the people in a given population, they must rely on a sample of participants from the wider population. The sample must be as representative as possible of the wider population, otherwise the generalisability of the findings to the wider population will be reduced. There are a number of sampling techniques from which the researcher can choose; these include *random sampling*; *quota sampling*; and *opportunity sampling*.

Random sampling

Random sampling is a technique whereby participants are chosen from the wider population using some random method, which can range from the flip of a coin to computer-generated random selection. Random sampling is seen as a very good method for achieving a representative sample, and is sometimes referred to as "probability sampling" because everyone in the wider population has an equal chance of being selected for inclusion in the sample. However, random sampling does have its limitations: for example, it can be time-consuming, and those who are selected for the sample might refuse to participate when asked.

Quota sampling

Quota sampling is a technique whereby the researcher chooses a sample that reflects the makeup, in numerical terms, of the wider population (Cozby, 1989). So, for example, if a researcher wanted to study gender differences in first-year undergraduate psychology students, and the wider population comprised a 60%/40% split females/males, then the sample must be comprised of this same ratio of females to males. Thus, in a sample population of say, 100 participants, the sample would contain 60 females and 40 males. This quota system can also be used for other factors, such as age, ethnic background, etc. Like all techniques, quota sampling does have its drawbacks. For example, it can be time-consuming and the researcher would still need to consider exactly how the subgroups that make up the sample are selected: e.g. what if those who are selected refuse to participate—how might this affect how representative the sample is?

Opportunity sampling

Opportunity sampling is a technique whereby participants are selected purely on the basis of their availability at that particular time. So, for example, if a third-year undergraduate walks into a canteen and asks those in the canteen if they would be willing to participate in an experiment and they agree, this would constitute an opportunity sample. It would be an opportunity sample because the people had been selected purely on the basis that they happened to be in the canteen at that particular time. This approach is least likely to produce a representative sample, but is a sampling procedure commonly used by undergraduate students. The approach also has a number of drawbacks to it, not least of which is the problem of just how representative the sample is to the wider population. These issues should be borne in mind when using such a sample and should be considered when discussing any findings from a study based on this type of sample.

The sampling method used for selecting participants for a study is very important and should be considered when planning the study, as well as in any subsequent critical consideration of the findings (e.g. in an experimental write-up). For further consideration of a range of sampling techniques see, for example, Breakwell et al. (1995, Part II); Cozby (1989, Chapter 8); Elmes et al. (1995, Chapter 5); Robson (1993, Part II); Robson, 1994. Once the sampling technique has been decided, the researcher must then decide which method to adopt. These methods include the *experimental method,* the *quasi-experimental approach, non-experimental methods,* and *qualitative approaches*, each of which is considered here briefly.

THE EXPERIMENTAL METHOD

The experimental method offers perhaps the most rigorous approach to testing a hypothesis or set of hypotheses. This approach incorporates the following key components:

- The formation of a hypothesis(es)
- Testing the hypothesis(es) in a controlled environment
- The manipulation of one or more independent variables
- The measurement of one or more dependent variables
- The specification of a particular design of the experiment
- The inclusion of at least one control and one experimental condition
- The inclusion of control procedure(s) in order to overcome potential confounding factors
- A causal inference drawn from the findings

The hypothesis

As stated earlier, a hypothesis is a statement about what is likely to occur between two or more factors in the experiment. For example, if you expect that watching televised violence will lead to increased aggression in the viewers, this could form a hypothesis that you wish to test. A null hypothesis is always that there will be no link between two factors. For example, "There will be no link between televised violence and levels of aggression in viewers" would constitute a null hypothesis.

The independent and dependent variables

The independent variable (IV) refers to some factor that is manipulated by the experimenter. This factor can have two or more levels—normally an *experimental condition* and a *control condition*. An experimental condition is where the participants receive some form of experimental manipulation or intervention: this is usually the group in whom the hypothesised change is expected to take place. The control condition is the counterpart to the experimental condition, and is labelled "control" because it is where the participants do not receive any experimental manipulation. Its inclusion provides a base-line measure of performance. Having both conditions enables the researcher to assess any change in performance across conditions, as measured in the dependent variable. The dependent variable (DV) refers to some measure of performance in the participants of the study.

Experimental design

The notion of design in research refers to the specific organisation or plan of a study: the relationship between the participants and the conditions (e.g. whether or not each participant performed in all the conditions); and the number and type of variables under consideration in the study. Broadly speaking, designs are divided into three types: *between-subjects*, *within-subjects*, and *mixed designs*.

A *between-subjects design* is one in which participants are assigned to either the experimental or control condition—but not to both. Where there are more than two conditions, again the principal is that each participant is assigned to only one of these conditions. This type of design is also known as an independent-groups design. Assignment to one or other of the groups can be based on *simple random assignment*. This is where each participant is assigned to a group based purely on chance; e.g. the flip of a coin. Assignment to a relevant condition can also be based on *matched random assignment*. This is where pairs of participants are matched on some important feature(s) (e.g. intelligence) and each one in that pair is assigned to a different condition—either the control or the experimental condition. The advantages of using such a design includes the fact that no carry-over effects occur (considered below under the confounding variables section). The disadvantages of using this design include an increase in the number of participants needed for the study and the possibility of some individual variation between conditions.

A *within-subjects design* is where each participant performs in all of the conditions—the experimental and control conditions. It is also known as a repeated-measures design. There are a number of advantages to using such a design: it lowers the number of participants needed for the study, and the use of the same participants across conditions reduces the possibility of individual variation between conditions. Potential problems with this design include the possibility of order effects (considered below under the confounding variables section).

A *mixed design* is where there is at least one between-subjects factor and one within-subjects factor incorporated into the experimental design. This is a more complex design than those outlined above and provides a good method for testing the potential interaction between two variables. For example, providing practice versus no-practice (this could be the between-subjects variable), and assessing what effect this has on students' performance in two different modes of assessment, examinations and coursework (this could be the within-subjects variable). When using such a design one must incorporate all the relevant control procedures (considered in the following section).

Confounding variables and control procedures

In addition to the IV and DV, there is a third class of variable that needs to be considered in research; that is, the confounding variable or factor. A confounding variable is one that exerts its influence in terms of its having a differential effect on the control and experimental conditions; that is, it has an effect on one condition and not the other. Such confounding occurs when the researcher fails to control for extraneous variables that can affect the performance of the participants in one part of the experiment.

An example would be where the aim of the experiment is to test adults' short-term memory for words, with the independent variable being mode of presentation (visual or auditory presentation) and the dependent variable being the amount of words recalled immediately after presentation was completed. If the length of the words (measured in syllables) was not controlled for, this might introduce a confounding factor into the experiment: for example, if participants in the visual presentation condition received a majority of three-syllable words, whereas the participants in the auditory condition received a majority of one-syllable words, then this might be a confounding factor. Any difference in recall may not be due to the type of presentation (visual or auditory), but might be confounded by the fact than one group received longer words—which are harder to recall than shorter words. When this occurs the internal validity of the experiment is open to question; i.e. the experimenter cannot be sure which factor has caused the change in performance: is it the experimental manipulation or the confounding variable? There are a number of techniques developed to overcome or reduce potentially confounding factors; these include *matching, randomisation,* and *counterbalancing.*

Matching is where participants in the experimental and control conditions are matched on a factor, or range of factors, that the experimenter suspects is likely to affect the scores on the dependent variable. Matching is a useful control measure where a between-subjects design is used. Thus, in a problem-solving task, it would be possible to match participants in terms of intelligence (Robson, 1994).

Randomisation refers to a technique whereby the researcher assigns participants to one condition or the other in a random fashion, and is therefore used in a between-subjects design. Thus, participants may be chosen at random to serve in either the experimental or the control condition. Randomisation assures that any extraneous variable is just as likely to affect one condition as it is the other condition. This technique ensures that the characteristic composition of the two groups is likely to be very similar (Cozby, 1989).

Counterbalancing is used in a within-subjects design in order to overcome order effects. An order effect can occur when participants are required to perform in two or more conditions. This can lead to a number of possible extraneous effects. For example, there may be a learning or "carry-over" effect in that some participants' performance may be affected in a later condition by their having participated in an earlier condition. Counterbalancing basically refers to developing some system whereby participants are randomly assigned different orders of carrying out the different treatment conditions, so that any order effect is balanced out (Robson, 1993). Thus, the first participant might receive the conditions in one particular order, whereas the next participant might receive the conditions in another order, and so on.

Causal inference and the experimental method

In a well-controlled experiment, where the researcher has manipulated the independent variable, has adequately controlled for confounding (or "nuisance") variables, and has predicted the direction in which a change should take place, then there is a very plausible argument for claiming that a change in the dependent variable is due to the experimental manipulation. The ability of the experiment to ascertain a causal relationship (that A caused B) is its big advantage over other techniques (Robson, 1994). The probability of this relationship between the IV and the DV being a true reflection of what happened in the experiment can be measured using appropriate statistical analysis (considered later in the section on data and statistical analysis).

THE QUASI-EXPERIMENTAL METHOD

The quasi-experimental approach to the study of behaviour has been defined as one which "attempts to liberalise the experiment to cope more realistically with conditions outside the laboratory" (Robson, 1993, p.47). This means that the quasi-experiment is an attempt to reproduce characteristics of the experimental approach outside the laboratory, in a "real-world" setting. In practice, this approach is useful in situations where true random allocation of participants to relevant conditions cannot be ensured. This approach incorporates the following key components:

- A formal literature search, as outlined earlier in this chapter
- The formation of a research question(s) or hypothesis(es)
- The use of methodology outside the strict laboratory situation

- The approximation of control features incorporated into the experimental method, so that the researcher can infer that a given treatment did have its intended effect (Cozby, 1989)
- A causal inference can be made

There are a number of quasi-experimental designs from which the researcher can choose. Those most commonly used include: the *non-equivalent control group pre-test–post-test design*; a *time series design*; or a *control series design*.

The non-equivalent control group pre-test–post-test design

This design incorporates an experimental and control group, each of which is tested prior to some treatment/manipulation stage (the pre-test phase) and after the treatment/manipulation stage (the post-test phase). The experimental group receives the actual manipulation, whereas the control group does not—this would constitute the independent variable. The actual measure(s) taken at the pre- and post-test stages (for both groups) would constitute the dependent variable. This design is called non-equivalent groups because it allows the researcher to select the separate samples for experimental and control groups on a non-random basis (e.g. a group of smokers and a group of non-smokers). This could be seen as a weakness in the design, but is acceptable because the design allows the researcher to *observe any changes from pre- to post-manipulation/treatment stages within the same group* (i.e. control pre-post; and experimental pre-post). Since there is a manipulation taking place (in terms of the IV) this design allows the researcher to argue that any change across pre-post stages is due to the manipulation itself.

This design can be particularly useful when testing variables that do not lend themselves easily to experimental manipulation in a laboratory setting (for example, intelligence, smoking behaviour, aggression, etc.). However, it does have its drawbacks. One problem with this design is the possibility of some sample selection bias entering the study (e.g. On what basis were the particular participants recruited for the study? Did they participate for any particular reason, such as those in the experimental group wanting the treatment/manipulation? What of those who refused?). Thus, the researcher has to be aware of possible cohort effects: those people in the control group might be quite different from those in the experimental group. Another drawback is the possibility of subject mortality, a term which refers to participants leaving the study for whatever reason.

The time series design

The time series design involves testing only one sample or group of participants—those who receive some treatment or manipulation, but involves testing these people over an extended period of time. Usually, this means assessing/testing them on several occasions (at least three times)—therefore measuring the dependent variable on several occasions before and after the manipulation has taken place (e.g. a number of times before and after a drug treatment has been given). The idea here is to gauge what effect the manipulation/treatment has had on the participants' psychological state/behaviour (e.g. Has there been a significant improvement in biological function? Has their behaviour changed?). Typically, the researcher will use multiple measures of psychological phenomena—but always administering the same assessments each time the participants are tested.

The main advantage with using this design is that it can reduce the sample bias that can occur when using two different groups. It can also provide a powerful argument for any changes that take place being due to the manipulation—since it involves the same participants being tested on each occasion. The major disadvantages with this design includes the possibility of a "testing effect" (i.e. it is possible that the participants become more adept at the assessments with practice); problems with subject mortality; fatigue and boredom effects; and "instrumentation effects" (see, for example, Breakwell et al., 1995).

The control series design

The control series design is really a combination of the previous two designs: it has elements of both. It includes a time series analysis; that is, multiple measures are taken before and after a given treatment/manipulation has taken place; but it also includes both an experimental group and a control group. This design has the advantage of having both an experimental and control group, as well as the opportunity to observe changes across pre- and post-manipulation stages within each group. This allows the researcher to make inferences about any changes that occur. The problems with this design include many of those previously outlined earlier, including subject mortality, possible instrumentation effects, and so on.

Although referred to here as "designs", quasi-experimental techniques should be seen as somewhat flexible approaches to studying psychological phenomena that cannot easily be tested using a strict experimental approach, rather than rigid designs that should be followed by the researcher. Many researchers adopt a combination of techniques that fall under the heading "quasi-experimental". For further reading on quasi-experimental approaches, see, for example, Aronson, Ellsworth, Carlsmith, and Gonzales (1990); Breakwell et al. (1995); Cozby (1989); Elmes et al. (1995); Kantowitz, Roediger III, and Elmes (1994); Robson (1993).

THE NON-EXPERIMENTAL METHOD

The non-experimental method offers a way of assessing non-manipulative factors, or phenomena that are naturally occurring (Cozby, 1989). Such an approach can be used to provide a description of the phenomena under study, or can be used to study the relationship between factors. This approach incorporates the following key components:

- A formal literature search as outlined earlier in the chapter
- The formation of a research question(s)
- Sampling procedures, such as: random, quota, and opportunity sampling
- A more naturalistic and less contrived approach to studying behaviour; i.e. no manipulation of variables
- A number of approaches including: observations, case studies, surveys, and the correlational method
- A causal inference cannot be drawn from the findings

The formation of research questions

Since non-experimental methods do not typically involve the manipulation of variables, often they will not involve the specification of experimental hypotheses. There may be an overall research aim or statement that is to be verified. As with other approaches, a literature search can provide the basis for the overall aim/statement the researcher wishes to address using a non-experimental approach. The major non-experimental approaches included here are: *observational methods, case studies, surveys*, and the *correlational approach*.

Observational method

Observational methods are ones in which the researcher observes naturally occurring behaviour outside the laboratory setting. Typically, such observations take place over an extended period of time. This approach can involve *non-participant* or *participant* observation.

Non-participant observation is where the researcher remains an outsider to the group she or he is studying and observes naturally occurring behaviour in that group. Therefore, the researcher does not become an active participant in the situation under study. The advantage with this specific approach is that because the researcher is "on the outside" she or he can observe the phenomena objectively and impartially. Where *participant observation* is used, the researcher becomes very much an active member of the group to be studied, observing the phenomenon as it occurs from inside the group itself. The advantage of this approach is that the researcher can study the phenomenon "from the inside and as it naturally occurs", often gaining access to groups that otherwise would be difficult to observe. With either approach, there are considerations that have to be borne in mind. With *non-participant* observation, the researcher has to consider the exact method to be used to observe things. For example, does the researcher conceal her or himself from view? And, if so, what implications might this have on the ethics of the approach, such as an invasion of privacy? On the other hand, being an active *participant* of the group under study might mean that the researcher loses her or his objectivity, and thus the whole validity of their findings might be adversely affected.

Once an overall approach has been decided on, and sufficient consideration has been given to the advantages and/or disadvantages of the approach, the researcher then has to decide on the precise method used for data collection. Typically, these include: *case studies; interviews; surveys;* or *correlational methods*, each of which is considered here briefly.

Case studies

A case study is often described as the study of an individual or small group of individuals with a view to studying their history, characteristic behaviours, reactions to given situations, and responses to particular manipulations (e.g. drug treatment) (Cozby, 1989, p.39). However, in a wider sense, it can also be used to refer to a strategy for carrying out research involving an empirical study of a contemporary phenomenon within its real-world context (Robson, 1993, pp. 51–53). In this latter sense, a case study can refer to the scientific study of an individual, a given situation, a group, or some other phenomenon. A case study therefore focuses on the development of a strategy for studying some phenomenon within its context, and the use of multiple techniques for collecting evidence about the case. It also involves an interpretation of findings in relation to the context and other issues, such as issues of validity, what generalisations can be made from the findings, and so on (see, for example, Robson, 1993).

A case study can consist of, for example, an individual being monitored on a single characteristic or a whole range of characteristics; or it can consist of, for example, the study of several individuals in a series of single-case studies. An example of the former scenario might be where a clinician studies the effects of a particular treatment on a patient. For example, the clinician might observe certain behaviour before treatment; during the course of the treatment; and after the removal of the treatment (as is the case with an A-B-A design). An example of the latter might be where several individuals are assessed, each of whom may be suffering from a similar condition (say, for example, some brain pathology).The aim of such a study might be to test a particular approach to rehabilitation—as is the case with a number of areas, such as the study of amnesia (see, for example, Barlow & Hersen, 1987; Kazdin, 1992; Solso & Johnson, 1994). The main advantage of using a case study approach is that the researcher can look at a particular individual or phenomenon in depth, obtaining a multitude of information about the case. The major disadvantage with this approach is in the lack of generalisability of the results to the wider population, though this, of course, depends on why the researcher has chosen to use the case study approach.

Surveys

Surveys generally refer to a group of techniques for gathering information from large numbers of people. The survey method is often used to gather data on people's opinions about certain phenomena (e.g. smoking habits, preference for particular brand names, voting behaviour, etc.), but can also be used to gauge specific attitudes, personality characteristics, and so on. This approach often involves assessing large numbers of participants (hundreds, or even thousands in some cases) and typically the methods used include: *interviews, attitude scales*, and *questionnaires* (see e.g. M.W. Eysenck, 1996; Oppenheim, 1992). So what are interviews, attitude scales, and questionnaires?

Interviews

An interview generally refers to a conversation between two persons, which is aimed at one person extracting information from the other. Researchers use interviews to find out about people's attitudes, opinions, habits, and so on. Within this general framework, the three main types of interview are: the *completely structured interview*; the *semi-structured interview*; and the *unstructured interview*.

The *completely structured interview* is where the researcher asks a series of predetermined questions and records the interviewee's responses on a standardised response sheet. Thus, the topics, precise questions, and response sheet are all produced in advance, and the researcher will keep to a strict agenda. The *semi-structured interview*, as the title suggests, is where some predetermined structure is used. The researcher might use a series of predetermined questions, but could deviate from those questions if she or he decides (during the interview) that there is some other, interesting, line of enquiry to pursue. Normally the researcher will record the interviewee's responses. Any changes the interviewer makes will be based on her or his perception of the situation (the interview) as it unfolds. The more experienced the interviewer, the better the semi-structured interview will be. Finally, the *unstructured interview* refers to a situation where there is no set agenda, it does not have a series of predetermined questions, but might consist of the researcher freely pursuing a number of topics with the interviewee.

Together, completely structured, semi-structured, and unstructured interviews are the most commonly used forms of the interview process. Interviews can be very useful in that they can be flexible and adaptive methods for discovering things about a given sample of people (for example, not only their verbal responses, but also their non-verbal behaviour can be recorded). On the other hand, they can be very time-consuming and some people find them intrusive (which might affect their willingness to participate, thus affecting how representative the sample might be). For further reading on a range of interview techniques, information recording techniques, validity and reliability issues/techniques, as well as interpretation of interview "data", see, for example, Breakwell et al., 1995; Elmes et al., 1995; Oppenheim, 1992; Robson, 1993.

Attitude scales

Attitudes are concepts used to describe the way in which a person thinks, feels, or behaves towards a particular object or situation. Since attitudes are essentially hypothetical constructs, measuring them inevitably involves using indirect measures, from which the researcher infers a given attitude to an object/situation. One way of measuring such constructs is by using attitude scales.

An attitude scale typically consists of sets of statements or series of words, which assess an individual's liking or disliking for a particular object or situation, or series of the same. Depending upon their responses, the researcher can place each individual somewhere along a particular point on the scale, representing their degree of positive or negative feelings towards the given attitude focus. The precise types of scales differ depending upon a number of things, such as the items used in the scale, but most scales will approximate to the well-established scales such as the Likert or the Thurstone scales. Only Likert scaling is considered here in greater detail; for Thurstone scaling the reader is referred to Cronbach (1990), Oppenheim (1992), and Robson (1993).

Likert scales, developed during the first half of this century, involve two essential aspects—the construction of the scale itself and the use of a scoring key. The procedure for the construction of the scale and the scoring key are as follows:

1. The collection of a large pool of positive and negative statements about the attitude object/situation.
2. The use of a standard scoring key. For positive statements, where the participant "strongly agrees" with the statement she or he is given a score of 5; where she or he "agrees" then a score of 4 is given; where she or he is "neutral" on the subject, a score of 3 is assigned; where she or he "disagrees" with the statement, then a score of 2 is given, and finally where she or he "strongly disagrees" with the statement, a score of 1 is given. For negative statements pertaining to the attitude object/situation, a reverse scoring mechanism is used. Thus, an overall positive/neutral/negative score can be assigned to each participant.
3. Administering the scale to a group of participants in order to gauge whether they have a positive or negative attitude towards the object/situation. This could constitute "piloting" the scale and could be used to test validity and reliability (two issues that are covered next).
4. Testing the scale for validity. Validity basically refers to how well the scale actually measures what it sets out to measure (i.e. positive or negative attitudes to the object/situation). For this, the researcher can use any one of a number of techniques, or a combination of these. These techniques include: *face validity, content validity, construct validity,* or *item analysis* (see e.g. Cronbach, 1990; Oppenheim, 1992; Robson, 1993).
5. Testing the scale for reliability. Reliability basically refers to the extent to which the attitude scale provides a consistent measure over time (i.e. does the same participant respond in a similar way when the same scale is administered again?). Again there are a number of ways this can be assessed, including *test-retest reliability,* and *split-half reliability* (see e.g. Cronbach, 1990; Oppenheim, 1992; Robson, 1993).
6. Once validity and reliability have been established, administering the scale to a group of participants in the main study.

Using attitude scales are useful ways in which the researcher can assess attitudes towards particular phenomena (for example, smoking, abortion, etc.). Attitude scales can also be used to look at wider issues such as how attitudes might be formed and prejudiced attitudes, as well as how these might be changed.

Questionnaires

Questionnaires are general techniques used in research to test current opinions and patterns of behaviour (Coolican, 1990). As with other survey methods, questionnaires can be used in quasi-experimental settings as well as in more naturalistic settings (e.g. field studies). The exact makeup of a questionnaire will depend upon a number of things such as: the aim(s) of the research, what precisely the researcher wishes to measure, and so on. Therefore, rather than giving the impression here that a single, precise format for questionnaire use is available, the rest of this section will consider the major features of questionnaire design. These are based on the key features outlined by Coolican (1990).

Minimise the information required from respondents. Keep the information required to a minimum and make the questions highly pertinent to the research topic. Avoid general "chit-chat" as this can be time-consuming, and avoid questions that are vague: the responses the researcher gets may vary simply because the nature of the question is open to different interpretations. Also, avoid asking unecessary questions, such as the sex of the respondent (unless, of course, it is not obvious (e.g. if the questionnaire was sent by post)).

Keep the questions fairly simple. Try to ensure that the questions used can be answered fairly easily. Do not include ones that might require a great deal of knowledge on the topic (unless the sample of respondents used are "experts" on a particular subject).

Choose questions that should produce truthful" answers. If the researcher chooses questions that the respondents might find difficult to answer entirely candidly, the responses may not be valid. For example, some people might find it difficult to be open about topics such as "Do you believe in smacking your child?", particularly if the political climate is one in which this is seen as unacceptable. Try to formulate questions that avoid such scenarios, or reassure the respondents that their views are entirely confidential, are not going to be judged, etc.

Ensure that the questions will be answered. Make sure that the questions used are such that they will ensure a response from the person who is being interviewed. Sensitive topics should be avoided or else the interviewee should be fully aware of the sensitive nature of the interview.

Use fixed and open-ended questions appropriately. Fixed questions refer to those that are designed in such a way that the respondent must choose one answer from a range of possible answers. An open-ended question is one which can be answered in whatever way the respondent wishes to answer. Fixed questions are useful because they can be easily coded and numerically analysed. Open-ended questions can be useful because the respondent can provide their own response, instead of choosing from a set of pre-determined responses, thus eliciting a more naturalistic response. Most questionnaires contain predominantly fixed questions, but many researchers also use open-ended questions.

For example, the following are fixed questions:
Question 1. Did you vote for the Labour Party at the last election?
Answer (circle one): Yes/No
Question 2. How may cigarettes do you smoke each week?
Answer (circle one)
a) between 1 and 20
b) between 20 and 40
c) between 40 and 60
d) 60 or more
e) I do not smoke cigarettes

For example, the following are open-ended questions:
Question 1. What are your views on abortion?
Question 2. How do you think the Chancellor of the Exchequer should handle the economy?

Like other forms of measurement, questionnaires should be tested for their discriminatory power. This means that they should be structured in such a way as to identify those individuals with extreme views, whilst not producing a wide range of scores in those people who are not at one extreme or the other. Also, as with other scales, questionnaires should be tested for validity and reliability, and should be standardised, preferably via a pilot study or several pilot studies (see also Coolican, 1990; Oppenheim, 1992).

Correlational method

A correlation basically refers to the *degree of association* between two factors. To take an example from Chapter 1, if a researcher wished to study the relationship between viewing violent television programmes and levels of overt aggression in children, they might use a correlational method to establish whether the two factors (i.e. viewing violent television programmes and overt aggression) are linked. Thus, if the researcher found that, as the amount of violent tv viewing increased, so did levels of overt aggression in child viewers, then they could say the two are correlated. It is worth noting that the correlational approach/

method is quite different from an experimental approach. This is because in an experiment the researcher manipulates a variable and predicts a change in behaviour: thus a *causal link* can be established. With a correlation it is quite different: the researcher can look only at the degree of association between two factors—not knowing exactly which factor caused a change in the other (e.g. is it that violent tv viewing leads to increased aggression? or do aggressive people watch violent tv?). *Thus, with a correlation, no causal link can be drawn.*

The association itself is assessed in terms of the *nature* and the *degree* of association. The nature of the association refers to whether a systematic change taking place in one factor is related to any systematic change taking place in another factor. For example, a positive correlation is where an increase in levels of one factor accompanies an increase in levels of another factor. The degree of association refers to a numerical estimate of how well associated the two factors are. For example, are the measured increases in one factor incrementing by the same amount as the measured increases in another factor? Both of these types of information can be established by the use of relevant correlational statistics and are reflected in the correlation coefficient (see, for example, Clegg, 1990; Greene & D'Oliveira, 1990; Robson, 1994).

There are a number of advantages to using a correlational approach, for example, the fact that the researcher can look at factors that do not easily lend themselves to experimental manipulation (for example, intelligence, smoking behaviour, etc.). Also, this approach often involves assessing large numbers of participants—a task which would be very time-consuming if they had to be tested in a laboratory setting. There are, however, disadvantages, not least of which is the inability to draw any causal link between factors (i.e. just because two factors are associated, it does not mean that one caused a change in the other; it could be that a third factor has affected them both). (For good coverage on the correlational method/approach and related statistical analysis, see, for example, Breakwell et al., 1995; Clegg, 1990; Elmes et al., 1995; Greene & D'Oliveira, 1990; Robson, 1994.)

DATA, STATISTICAL ANALYSIS, AND CAUSAL INFERENCE

Although there are instances in research that do not require the formal measurement of psychological phenomena (as is the case with a number of qualitative research paradigms), there are many instances where measurement of data is desirable (as is the case in all quantitative research). Measurement basically refers to the numerical classification and manipulation of some phenomenon(a). The precise method of measurement is dictated by particular sets of rules (i.e. a particular statistical procedure and its underlying philosophy). Since psychological phenomena are not normally open to direct measurement, it is often the case that indirect measures are used to classify and quantify such phenomena. Statistics are applied to the data collected so that the researcher can *describe* the data collected and *make inferences* about that data (Cozby, 1989). Statistics are techniques that enable the researcher to identify characteristics of a sample of data drawn from a larger population. Thus, statistics can be used to summarise, describe, calculate differences between, and demonstrate associations between, sets of sample data.

Since the realms of statistical theory, the procedures for applying them, and the precise outputs that are produced by them, could fill volumes of texts, and since the precise statistical procedure depends upon many aspects of the study (e.g. the precise aims of the research, the design, the number of factors/variables, etc.), an exhaustive trawl of statistical procedure will not be carried out here. What will be considered are three important aspects that enable the researcher to judge which statistical procedures are most applicable to the data she or he collects. These aspects are: the *level of measurement* used; the distinction between *parametric and non-parametric tests*; and the distinction between *descriptive and inferential statistics*. A flow-chart of the major statistical tests used in psychological research is presented at the end of this section. It should be noted that as you progress through the first two years of study on a research methods course, many more issues in relation to methods and statistics (other than those considered here) may be covered.

Levels of measurement

Levels of measurement are ways in which the researcher can classify raw data, before going on to decide what statistical tests can be applied in order to make sense of the data. Thus, different levels of measurement will produce different types of data, which in turn will affect the types of statistical analysis(es) open to the researcher. Generally, there are four levels of measurement/types of data. These are: *nominal, ordinal, interval,* and *ratio*. So how do these differ?

Nominal level data.   A nominal level of measurement is where the researcher categorises information by placing it into one category or another. For example, where the researcher is interested in looking at what frequency of male and female students fall into either the mature or non-mature student categories (mature traditionally being over the age of 21 upon entry to a university). The items are grouped together on some characteristic or set of characteristics (e.g. gender and entry status), producing simple, nominal data. Nominal data can include several categories of information which can be given arbitrary labels (e.g. categories 1, 2, 3; or A, B, C, etc.)—*but these do not represent any differences in size of the data*: i.e. category 3 is not three times greater than category 1. The numbers that fall into the relevant categories are referred to as frequencies (e.g. 12 male mature students/8 female mature students, and so on).

The nominal level of measurement presents the least amount of quantitative information (Coolican, 1990) and therefore places limitations on the types of statistical analyses that can be carried out on that data. Thus, the researcher can describe relative frequencies of occurrence, but cannot test for differences in performance between, say, females and males, matures and non-matures, etc.

Ordinal level data.   An ordinal level of measurement involves the use of some type of ordered scale; categories of information can be placed at some point along that scale in an ordered fashion. Ordinal data refers to numbers that are placed on that scale in order of preference, with the implication that one category is "better" or "worse" than another category. So, for example, if a lecturer were to order her or his students on a scale of ability using categories such as very good, good, medium, bad, very bad, this would constitute an ordinal measure because it involves rank ordering the information. However, one drawback of an ordinal level of measurement is that the intervals between scale points (i.e. the categories themselves) cannot be assumed to be equal in value. So, for example, those students falling into the very good category cannot be assumed to be five times better than those falling into the very bad category. The nature of ordinal data places limitations on the statistical analyses that can be applied to the data.

Interval level data.   An interval level of measurement is one that "assumes equal intervals between the data on a continuous numerical scale" (Greene & D'Oliveira, 1990, p.26). What this entails, then, is data that is numerical in form, is measured along some continuum or scale, and has equal intervals between each scale point, such as the Fahrenheit temperature scale. One thing to remember about interval data is that it does not have to have a zero starting point, as, for example, with Fahrenheit temperature. Because interval scales require numerical data and because the differences between each point on the scale represents equal distance, interval level data can be subjected to more complex statistical analyses than can nominal or ordinal data.

Ratio level data.   A ratio level of measurement is where there is an exact zero starting point to the scale (e.g. as in the case of some memory tests), but it is the same as interval data in all other respects. This exact zero starting point would be meaningful if the researcher were, for example, testing pulse rate in humans (a zero pulse rate might well be important to the researcher!). Since the greatest difference between interval and ratio levels of measurement is the fact that the latter has a zero starting point, the statistics that can be applied are the same in either case. Thus, many researchers do not distinguish between the two types of data for statistical purposes.

Parametric and non-parametric tests

Parametric tests are ones which make assumptions about the population from which the sample is drawn. The data obtained from an experiment or study should meet these assumptions before parametric statistics can be applied to the data. These are:

1.   The data itself should be at least interval level data.
2.   The amount of variability in each data set should be similar. This is known as homogeneity of variance.
3.   Each sample set of data should be a normal distribution.

Strictly speaking, if these criteria are not met, then parametric statistical tests should not be used. The advantage of using parametric tests includes the fact that they are powerful tests. Power refers to the ability of the test to detect experimental effects from the data that is produced; the more powerful the test the greater its ability to detect an effect that is present (Elmes et al., 1995). The power of a statistical test can be affected by other factors as well, such as the size of the sample—the greater the sample size, the greater the likelihood of detecting an effect. Where one or more of these assumptions cannot be met (say, for example, the data is only nominal level) then the researcher should use a non-parametric test.

Non-parametric tests are, by definition, ones which can be used on data that do not meet the assumptions for parametric testing, and are sometimes referred to as "distribution-free tests". These can be useful in situations where, for example, the researcher has collected very simple data (e.g. data based on categories [nominal data]). Non-parametric tests lack the power ascribed to the parametric tests, but are equally acceptable forms of statistical testing.

Descriptive and inferential statistics

Descriptive statistics are ways in which the data yielded from an experiment or study can be summarised. This is why they are also referred to as "summary statistics". Descriptive statistics include those that describe the most typical value—as measured by some averaging procedure—and those that describe the amount of variability in a set of data. These two classes of statistics are known as *measures of central tendency*, and *measures of dispersion*. Usually, a researcher will choose only one measure from each class (typically the mean and standard deviation) per set of data, since these two measures can tell you what trends are emerging in the data and how widely dispersed the data is around the mean.

Measures of central tendency refer to those sets of statistics that describe the average of a set of data and include *the mean, the mode, and the median. The mean* represents the average score for a set of data and is calculated simply by dividing the total of a set of data by the number of numbers in that set of data. The mean can provide a good indication of the typical value in a set of data, particularly when there is not a great deal of dispersion in the data (i.e. all the numbers are clustered closely together)—but can be thrown out by extreme scores entering the data set. Having said this, the mean is the most frequently used descriptive statistic in psychology and is thought to be the most representative of the average of a set of data. *The median* is a way of establishing what the central value is in a given data set. This can be estimated by arranging the numbers in the data set in ascending order of size and seeing which number appears in the central point: this is said to be the median. Using this procedure can be time-consuming and the median can be affected by a change in any number near the central point itself (whereas the mean is not). *The mode* simply refers to the most frequently occurring number (or score) in a given data set and, in this sense, it provides some measure of the most typical value in the data set. You can have a bi-modal distribution (where there are two numbers appearing with equally high frequency), or a tri-modal situation (three modes), and so on. The major drawback with the mode is that it can vary greatly with the introduction of few numbers to the data set; it is said to be unstable, and is rarely used in psychological research. (For further reading, see Clegg, 1990; Coolican, 1990; Greene & D'Oliveira, 1990; Robson, 1994.)

Measures of dispersion provide summary information about the spread of numbers or scores in a given data set and should be used in conjunction with one of the descriptive statistics. There are three commonly used measures of dispersion: these are *the range, the mean deviation*, and *the standard deviation*. *The range* gives the researcher some idea of the spread of scores within the data set and represents the difference between the lowest and highest scores in that data, described in a single number (the higher this number, the greater the range is for the data). The range is useful when the scores in the data set are clustered closely together, but can be thrown out by extreme scores in the data. *The mean deviation* is calculated by estimating how many points each number or score is away from the mean (the mean deviations). A total of these mean deviations is calculated and then divided by the total number of numbers in the data set, thus giving a mean deviation across the data set. The higher the mean deviation, the greater the spread of scores. The mean deviation is rarely used in psychological reports because it ignores some of the mathematical properties of data sets (for example, it does not take into account pluses or minuses). *The standard deviation* again estimates the spread of scores from a central point (the mean), but also takes into account positive and negative numbers—an advantage over the mean deviation. This is achieved by using a different statistical procedure, which has more powerful mathematical properties than the formula for the mean deviation. (For further reading see, for example, Clegg, 1990; Coolican, 1990; Greene & D'Oliveira, 1990; Robson, 1994.)

Inferential statistics are a branch of statistical procedures which allow the researcher to "present the probability of whether the observed differences between the various experimental [and control] conditions have been produced by random, or chance, factors." (Elmes et al., 1995, p.82). What this means is that inferential statistics can tell the researcher whether any differences in the results (which can often be intimated by trends in the data) are effects due to the manipulation, or whether chance cannot be ruled out. Inferential statistics also estimate the probability of such results appearing again in future experiments of a similar kind (see Clegg, 1990; Coolican, 1990; Greene & D'Oliveira, 1990; Robson, 1994). For a range of the major inferential statistics used in psychological research, see the flow-chart following this section.

It should be noted here that before applying inferential statistics the researcher must first apply the necessary descriptive analyses to the data. Only by applying descriptive and inferential statistics can the researcher establish what trends are emerging from the data and whether these effects are significant or not.

A final note on data and statistics

Figure 4.1 contains an easy-to-follow flow-chart of the major statistical analyses used in psychology. These tests are classified according to the number of variables/factors in the study, the level of measurement used,

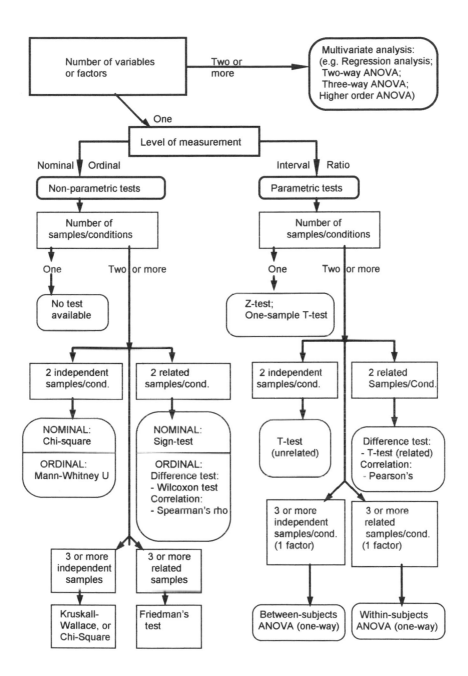

FIG. 4.1. Flow-chart of major statistical tests for psychology.

and the type of design of the study; and they are given with the parametric and equivalent non-parametric tests used. (For further reading on data, statistical formulae, and procedures, see, for example, Clegg, 1990; Coolican, 1990; Ferguson, 1981; Gravetter & Wallnau, 1996; Greene & D'Oliveira, 1990; Heiman, 1996; Hinkle, Wiersma, & Jurs, 1994; Robson, 1994).

QUALITATIVE APPROACHES

Qualitative approaches to the study of behaviour do not follow conventional modes of analysis like those apparent in the other methodologies, outlined previously (Robson, 1993). However, there are a number of characteristics that are key elements in qualitative research. These are:

- A formal literature search, as outlined earlier in the chapter
- The formation of a research question(s) that is to be addressed
- A method used for generating qualitative data
- A method used to code the data
- A method used to conduct some form of content analysis
- Some conclusion specific to the phenomenon under study

The literature search and formation of a research question(s)

This can involve a formal literature search, as described earlier in the chapter, and/or a pilot stage where the researcher formulates a research question or questions by observing some natural phenomenon she or he wishes to study. Typically, this will not involve a specific hypothesis(es), but can be a question, an overall aim, a focus point for the study, or multiples of all three. Often the research focus is flexible, in that it can change during the process of observing and assessing the phenomenon(a) under study.

The method for generating data

Once a particular research question or focus point has been decided on, the researcher will then decide what approach to studying the phenomenon(a) she or he will adopt. This refers to the methodology adopted by the researcher in order to gather data about the phenomenon(a) under study. Data, in the qualitative sense, does not necessarily refer to quantifiable amounts (although it can), rather it refers to the type of information gathered by the researcher. Such data can come in the form of language, non-verbal behaviour, or just about anything that is observable. The types of methods used for qualitative research vary, depending on the aims of the study, the nature of the study, etc. They can involve group study, as, for example, with participant or non-participant observation techniques, or they can be based on a single-case study method. Indeed, many of those approaches outlined earlier lend themselves to qualitative research.

Once a particular approach has been decided on, the researcher should, wherever possible, ensure that the approach is valid and reliable. Triangulation is one method used to achieve this. Triangulation is a technique whereby the data is assessed by using two (or more) methods of study in order to verify one's results. This can be problematic where the study is very time-consuming and takes place over an extended period of time (e.g. where there is an exhaustive amount of observation taking place, looking at several aspects of human functioning). Other methods of data collection include interviewing, questioning, discourse analysis, repertory grid techniques, Q-sorting, role-playing, focus groups, the study of archive data, and so on (see, for example, Breakwell et. al., 1995; Coolican, 1990; Robson, 1993).

Coding and analysing the data

Once the data has been collected, some method for coding it should be employed. Coding data refers to reducing it to some manageable form; for example, generating categories of information and assigning the data to one of these categories. Once coded, the data can be described in some way (for example, this could be an account in a narrative form of what has happened). Once the data has been coded and described, then some form of content analysis can be carried out in order to complete the analysis of the data. Content analysis is a technique that allows the researcher to analyse the information in terms of units (which can be words, characters, themes occurring in a narrative, etc.), and estimate the relative frequency of each source of information.

Conclusions drawn from qualitative research

Once the analyses have been carried out on the data, the researcher can then refer what she or he has found back to the research question or focus of the study. Typically, the conclusions drawn from qualitative research should be specific to the sample included in the study; and generalising to wider populations should be approached with caution. Like other approaches to research, a full report is normally written as a final stage to the research process.

For further reading on carrying out and writing up qualitative reports see, for example, Breakwell et al. (1995); Colman (1995b); Haworth (1996); Mason (1996); Robson (1993). There are also many texts on how to carry out and write up quantitative research projects (see Breakwell et al., 1995; Christenson, 1988; Colman, 1995; Elmes et al., 1995; Haworth, 1996; Jones, 1995; Robson, 1993; Shaughnessy & Zechmeister, 1994).

PART 2   ETHICS IN RESEARCH

Before carrying out a piece of research in psychology, there are a number of ethical considerations that a researcher must bear in mind when designing a study. Some brief notes on the subject are provided here, but for a full consideration of formal criteria on ethics in research the reader is referred to the British Psychological Society (BPS) (1990), *Ethics in psychological research and practice*, or the American Psychological Association (APA) (1990), *Ethical principles of psychologists*.

Ethical issues in research are to do with the way you conduct your research—the rights and wrongs. Psychologists are expected to conduct themselves in line with ethical guidelines that are set by bodies like the British Psychological Society and the equivalent American Psychological Association. Not only do you have a duty to protect the rights of the participants in your study, but also to protect the reputation of the discipline under which name you are studying, psychology. In most cases, given the types of research conducted by the majority of psychology students, the only ethical considerations you need to ensure are that your subjects have consented to their participation in the study and that they are fully debriefed. However, in some cases where there is a risk of harming or causing psychological distress, then the researcher needs to adhere to the guidelines. Here are some of the major ethical considerations for a researcher.

Considering the welfare of your participants

As a researcher you must ensure that the participants in your study are protected from physical harm or from suffering psychological harm as a result of your manipulation(s). In some cases there is inevitably a risk (e.g. if you were administering a drug—say, to a patient in care—which might have some side effects), in which case you must go through the relevant ethics committee associated with that particular institute. In short, it is your duty to ensure the safety of your participants.

Gaining the consent of the participants

Wherever possible, the researcher should ensure that all the participants are volunteers and have given their full consent. Some researchers have their participants sign a consent form before testing them. In some cases, gaining the consent of the individuals you wish to study is difficult (if not impossible), for example, if you want to study very young children in the school setting, or disturbed patients in a psychiatric hospital. In such cases consent can be obtained from those who are in authority over those persons. For example, the Head of the school may take responsibility for agreeing to your having access to test the children; or the Psychiatrist can give consent in the medical setting. It is a good idea to have a letter of introduction from your supervisor for the project: this offers some assurance to those outside your institute that your intentions are honourable and that you will conduct yourself in an appropriate manner.

Deceiving your participants

Deceiving your participants should be avoided whenever possible. The BPS (1990) suggests that deception should not be used if, once the participants have been debriefed, they are likely to have objected to the study had they been told about it beforehand. This is sometimes difficult to do because, as a researcher, you might argue that informing the participants of what you are going to do may well cause a change in naturally occurring behaviour. The general advice on this is that if you have to deceive your participants you should take the matter before some form of ethics committee and debrief your participants as soon as possible after the study is complete.

Debriefing your participants

You should always fully debrief your participants once they have participated in the research. This involves telling them the nature of the study, the aims, and what was found in the study. Indeed, you should be willing to tell the participants anything they wish to know about their participation in the study.

In addition, your participants should also have the following rights:

- *The right to withdraw from the study at any time:* forcing the person to take part in the study may reduce the validity of your results.
- *The right to anonymity and confidentiality:* you might "code" your participants instead of using their names, if this is possible.

See also Wadeley (1991) and Kimmel (1996) for further consideration of ethical issues and guidelines in relation to research.

PART 3   EMPIRICAL RESEARCH REPORT WRITING

Having conducted an experiment (or a non-experimental study) and analysed the data from it, the researcher is normally required to write a report on what the experiment was about; what the procedure was for carrying it out; what was found in the experiment; and a full explanation as to why the things occurred as they did during the experiment. Within the field of psychology, there are clear rules that have been developed for writing empirical reports. Such rules relate mainly to the particular format the empirical report should take, and should be adhered to by the report writer. Following a standard format for empirical report writing makes it easier for other researchers to comprehend the large numbers of research articles they are likely to access during the course of their work. It also allows report writers to get their ideas, procedures, and results across to others.

Although, as a general rule of thumb, empirical reports should follow the overall format of an article in a journal (see, for example, the *British Journal of Psychology*, the *British Journal of Developmental Psychology*, and the *American Journal of Psychology*), the types of reports written on an undergraduate degree course usually contain more detail than would be found in a journal article. For example, all the raw data is normally provided in an undergraduate practical, whereas they are not provided for a journal article. All too often, undergraduate students fail to provide a clear, coherent, or complete report and lose vital coursework marks as a result of an inadequate write-up of their work. So, again, the idea is to spend some time on writing the report before submitting it for marking. As previously suggested for essays, ask a fellow student to look at a draft of the report to check for any major omissions. You could reciprocate by doing the same for your fellow student.

What follows is a guide designed to cover the most important aspects of writing empirical reports within a psychological framework. Do bear in mind that this is meant as a piece of scientific writing and must be well-structured according to a standard format. This standard format is set out in the remainder of this chapter. Guidelines about the length of a practical report are normally provided to students on particular courses.

THE STRUCTURE OF THE REPORT

An empirical report is normally presented in a series of subsections, each of which begins with the title of the subsection as a heading. The relevant subsections are: the Title, Abstract, Introduction, Method, Results, Discussion, References, and Appendix. This is the order in which they are dealt with here. Appendix 2 contains an example of a completed write-up of an experiment and should be referred to in conjunction with these guidelines. Please note that for a second-year, and particularly for a final-year, undergraduate psychology project the length of the write-up will be much greater than the length of the report given as an example in Appendix 2. Generally, the average length of a second-year report is about 4000 to 5000 words, and a final-year project ranges from about 10,000 to 12,000 words. This means that, for example, the Introduction and Discussion sections for a final-year psychology project would include much more extensive coverage and/or expansion of relevant literature and related discussion points than is given here. Specific guidance as to the length of such a project and guidance on details, such as structure, will be provided by the project supervisor you are assigned in your final year. The final-year project is seen by many as the pinnacle of your degree and is likely to carry more marks than any other piece of work or exam. A final point that students should bear in mind is that any project write-up needs to be written in the third person (see Chapter 3 on writing style).

THE TITLE

The title itself should convey information about the main aspects of the experiment (or non-experimental study). It should briefly identify the following aspects of the study: the independent and dependent variables, or factors under study; the subject population; and what particular method was used. For example, consider the following title:

> The effects of overt rehearsal on recall in young and older
> children, using a serial recall task.

It conveys information about: the independent variable (the manipulation of overt rehearsal); the dependent variable (recall); the subjects (young and older children); and it mentions the particular methodological paradigm used (a serial recall task). The title will often be the first thing the reader encounters, so make it clear, short and informative. Finally, avoid using phrases such as "An experiment that tests ..." or "An investigation into ..."; these types of phrases are not specific enough and take up valuable word space that could be used to include additional information relevant to the project. The title page comes before the main body of the report and should typically contain information about the following:

Full name of researcher(s):
Year of study/Submission date:
Course/Module:
Name of supervisor:
Title of report:

General rules for the Title

1. Keep it short: try not to exceed about 15–20 words.
2. Include sufficient detail so that the reader has a good idea of the major focus of the experiment.
3. Do not include too much detail: report such detail in later sections.

ABSTRACT

This section is called the *Abstract* because it contains information that is abstracted from other parts of the report: it is also referred to as the *Summary*. Having an Abstract section at the beginning of the report is useful for those people wishing to assess whether your particular article/report is relevant to their needs. If the report appears to be relevant, the researcher can spend time reading the whole thing. Indeed, most computer-based literature searches provide only brief details about the author, source, and the Abstract, so it is important that this section of your article/report contains the essential details of your experiment. (If you go on to submit a research paper for, say, a conference, you will be asked to forward an abstract of the article you wish to present. If your abstract omits important details, your submission will be rejected. There are a number of undergraduate conferences each year where some final year students choose to submit their work.) The Abstract section should stand out from the rest of the report (indent it and use single-line spacing) and should be relatively brief (between 100 and 150 words). It should contain brief details about the following: the aim of the experiment; the citation of any major experiment and/or theory underlying the experiment; the hypothesis(es); general design features; a brief interpretation of results; and any overall conclusion(s) that have been reached. Thus, the Abstract will consist of brief details taken from the other major sections of the report—the Introduction, Method, Results, and Discussion.

Please note: Details from the Appendix section of the report are not normally included in an Abstract.

Although the Abstract appears as the first major subsection in the completed written report, it is often not written until the rest of the report has been completed. This is because it is easier to extract information about the experiment after you have put it all down on paper in a report form, rather than trying to wade through the sometimes vast amounts of information you have collected, such as notes on articles, printouts of results, etc.

General rules for Abstract
1. Keep it relatively brief: between 100 and 150 words.
2. Include the most important details from Introduction, Method, Results, and Discussion sections of the report.
3. Use single-line spacing and indent this section.
4. Compile the Abstract after you have written the bulk of the report.

INTRODUCTION

A researcher may carry out an experiment for any one of a number of reasons. It might be that the experiment is purely "experimental" in nature, in that no one else (at least to your knowledge) has looked at what effects a particular variable might have on another, or it might be a replication of a new and important finding, or, as is the case with most final-year undergraduate projects, it might be an attempt to extend support for some existing hypothesis(es) and/or theory by manipulating a number of conditions in some way. As students progress through their undergraduate course, more emphasis is placed on experimentation that extends the literature, rather than the mere replication of previous work.

Whatever the motivation for carrying out an experiment, few experiments are conducted without there being some background information available to guide hypothesis-making. Invariably, there will be a body of literature that is relevant to the experiment you wish to run. The Introduction should summarise relevant empirical and theoretical work done previously in the area under study. It should flow from a general consideration of the area, through to summaries of previous empirical and theoretical work related to the area (always concluding something about each piece of work), to a specific outline of the present experiment, and finally it should lead to a clear, concise set of statements about the hypothesis(es). In many ways, the Introduction sets the scene for the experiment itself. It is often seen as having a funnelling effect—going from the general, to the more specific sets of empirical and theoretical literature, and on to a very specific focus point in terms of the experimental hypothesis(es). The Introduction should also state what novel feature(s) there are in the experiment (if applicable).

Please note: A good introduction includes a *selection* of key references from the literature, not an enormous summary of all the literature you can find on the topic.

Some tutors prefer to see the Introduction split into two discrete sections: a *General literature review* that covers the general area and empirical/theoretical literature that is available, and a specific *Introduction to the experiment*, which specifically outlines the aims of the experiment, cites briefly any major studies relevant to the experiment, stresses any novel features of the experiment, and states the hypothesis(es) to be tested. As suggested, the Introduction should finish by stating what *experimental hypothesis(es)* are to be tested, as well as the *null hypothesis(es)*. These hypotheses should be stated clearly and independently of each other, under a relevant subheading. Any student who feels there might be some problem with regard to a tutor's preference for the precise format of the Introduction can easily check with the tutor beforehand.

General rules for Introduction

1. Move from a general consideration of the area to a more specific focus point of the experiment so that your Introduction has the so-called funnelling effect mentioned earlier in this section.
2. Provide summaries of theoretical and empirical literature relevant to the experimental paradigm.
3. Use historical and up-to-date material wherever possible, and provide link pieces between sections of the Introduction.
4. Point out any novel feature(s) to the experiment.
5. List the experimental hypothesis(es) (and, if appropriate, the null hypothesis[es]) at the end of the Introduction.

METHOD

The main aim of this section is to provide sufficient methodological detail about the experiment so that anyone who chooses to can evaluate the appropriateness of the method used in your experiment, or can easily replicate your experiment (or a part of your experiment) after reading your report. The Method section is subdivided into the following subsections: Design, Participants, Materials (and Apparatus), and Procedure. As well as having sufficient detail, the organisation (its structure) of this section is also important and influences the tutor's assessment of this part of the report: so do adhere to the structure outlined below (unless your tutor advises otherwise).

Design

This section should provide concise information about the following:

- The type of design used in the experiment (such as whether it was an independent groups or matched groups design, a repeated measures, a quasi-experimental design, a correlational design, or some other design)
- What constituted the independent variable(s), or factor(s) under study, and what the different levels of this were. For example, word length might be the independent variable, with two levels (long and short words)
- What constituted the dependent variable(s), or measures, with brief details of how this was measured. For example, total number of words recalled might be the dependent variable
- Details of what methods were used to deal with order effects (for example, was randomisation used, counterbalancing, etc?)
- Other control methods employed in the experiment (i.e. how the experimenter controlled for nuisance variables)

Participants

This section should provide brief details about the participant sample and should include details on the following:

- The total number of participants, including numbers per condition
- Age distribution: age range and mean age, per group
- Sex distribution: how many males/females per group
- Brief details of the population they were drawn from. For example, were they undergraduate students? If so, which course were they taking?
- Other relevant details. For example, were they chosen at random? Were they volunteers?

Materials (and Apparatus)

You should include here enough detail to enable the reader to reproduce (if they wish to) similar materials and apparatus for a future experiment. Give the relevant tradename of any apparatus used. If the apparatus is new or highly specialised, a diagram may be used to demonstrate such aspects. If this is rather detailed and is likely to take up much space, then it can be placed in an Appendix section at the back of the report and referred to appropriately. Exact descriptions of materials, such as word lists, must either be given here or in the Appendix section of the report and referred to appropriately in the Materials section. For example, you might write "See Appendix 1 for details of word lists".

Procedure

The overall rule of thumb here is simple: describe what typically happened to a participant during the running of the experiment. What you should have here is a standardised procedure. The following details should be provided in enough detail for a researcher to easily replicate your procedure:

- Details of how the stimuli were presented to the participant
- How the participants were expected to respond
- Details of the relevant timing procedures (e.g. what the rate of item presentation was; what the inter-stimulus-interval time was)
- Whether the participants were tested individually or in groups
- A verbatim account of standardised instructions given to a participant (but if the instructions are very lengthy, these may be placed in an Appendix and referred to appropriately here)
- What the differences in procedure were between the conditions
- Any other relevant detail; for example were the participants debriefed

Please note: The Procedure is the only section that includes detailed information about how the experiment was run. So make sure that you have included all of the above details. However, if you realise a flaw in your method/procedure *after* you have run the experiment, *do not discuss it here* (this is a common mistake made by undergraduate students). Leave any discussion of major flaws until the Discussion section.

General rules for Method

1. Subsection into Design, Participants, Materials (and Apparatus), and Procedure.
2. Provide sufficient detail so that the experiment can be replicated (in part or in whole) by another researcher.
3. Where the report writer feels there is too much detail (e.g. where several pages of exhaustive instructions have been used), put this information in an Appendix section and refer to it accordingly.
4. Do not discuss any flaws in the Design or Procedure here. Leave such discussion until the relevant Discussion section of the report.
5. Ensure that some other person could replicate the experiment on the basis of the details contained in this section.

RESULTS

In the Results section of the report, the data you have collected is summarised and the findings from relevant statistical analyses are reported. This section should include *descriptive statistics* and *inferential statistics*. Descriptive statistics allow you to present your data in a condensed form and describe trends emerging from that data. Thus, descriptive statistics are used to summarise the data so that a researcher reading your report can begin to understand what has actually happened as a result of running the Procedure (i.e. what the emerging trends were). Inferential statistics are a branch of statistics that allow the researcher to estimate whether the conditions created in the experimental method have actually caused a significant change in the performance of the participants. By inferring that the manipulation(s) in the experiment have had a significant effect on performance in the participants, the researcher can evaluate whether or not there is support for the experimental hypothesis(es). Please note that you do not discuss your findings here: that is the main purpose of the Discussion section that follows the results. Do not place your raw data in this section (raw data should be listed in a table in the Appendix section at the back of the report).

Descriptive statistics (also referred to as *summary statistics*), such as means and standard deviations, should be presented in a table (and usually in graph form), followed by a concise statement about the emerging trends in the descriptive statistics (e.g. how the mean of group A differs from the mean of group B). You *must not* infer whether or not a hypothesis has been supported on the basis of the descriptive statistics alone. (For examples of a descriptive table and graphs, see the practical write-up in Appendix 2.) Finally, the results of the inferential statistics applied to the data are reported. When reporting these in the Results section, report what test was used, what value was obtained from the statistic, the degrees of freedom (or some other appropriate figure) and the significance level. For example, part of a Results section might read as follows:

> For the adults, an independent *t*-test revealed significantly greater recall in the Control than in the Experimental condition [$t(30)=3.68, p < .05$]. Therefore, the null hypothesis can be rejected and the experimental hypothesis accepted.

Your Results section should not consist of pages and pages of computer printouts of statistics carried out on computer packages, such as SPSS printouts. Rather you should summarise the relevant parts of the analyses and present it here formally. Remember, you *must not* discuss your findings in detail in the Results section. Such discussion forms part of the content of the Discussion section that follows.

General rules for Results

1. Do not put raw data or full workings of statistical calculations in this section. These should be placed in an Appendix at the end of the report, labelled and referred to appropriately.
2. Descriptive statistics are a way of summarising the data obtained and must be included in this section (both in tabular and graph form), before a summary of the inferential statistics.
3. Inferential statistics allow you to state whether a hypothesis has been supported or not, and again, must be included in this section *after* you have presented the descriptive statistics.
4. All results should be briefly described in words, regardless of tables or graphs.
5. Briefly state what the relationship is between the results and the hypothesis(es) set out in the Introduction.
6. Do not discuss the results here. Such discussion should take place in the Discussion section that follows.

DISCUSSION

Having reported the findings from the experiment clearly and relatively concisely, the next step is to fully discuss your findings in relation to the relevant background literature and your specific hypothesis(es). The Discussion section should begin with a summary of the major findings in words, not repeating the figures from the previous section. These findings can then be related back to the consideration of the area, as set out in the Introduction. And, most importantly, to the specific hypothesis(es) set out there. Try to address questions like: Do the findings support the hypothesis(es)? Are the findings consistent with what other researchers in the area have found? If not, what are the major discrepancies between your findings and those from other researchers? Do the findings support a particular theory or model that might be dominant in the area? Can you identify any methodological shortcomings or flaws in the experiment? If there are flaws, how might these be rectified in future experiments? Finally, you should address two other issues in the Discussion section: Are there any recommendations you can make for future research on this topic? Have your findings any implications for existing theory/research, or are they applicable in some way? Your Discussion can finish by stating some overall conclusion(s) about the experiment.

General rules for Discussion

1. Provide a written summary of the findings.
2. Relate the findings back to the hypothesis(es) set out in the Introduction.
3. Interpret the findings in relation to the literature in the Introduction (both theory and research).
4. Consider any shortcomings or flaws of the experiment, and make suggestions about improvements in design, procedure, etc.
5. Assess what implications and/or applications your findings might have in relation to the phenomenon/topic under consideration.
6. Make sensible suggestions for future research.
7. Draw the discussion to a close with some conclusion(s).

Please note: The Discussion section is seen by many tutors as the most important section because it is your critical analysis of the experiment as a whole; and it is therefore likely to carry the most marks. So do spend some time getting it right.

REFERENCES

In the Introduction and Discussion sections of the report, you will have referred to a number of pieces of published work. All references cited in the report should be listed here. Your Reference section must come immediately following the Discussion section of the report, before the Appendices. In the Reference section, details of all publications referred to in the other sections of the report should be listed in alphabetical order of author. For the specific format references should take, see Chapter 3.

APPENDICES

An Appendix is a section within which you can place very detailed information that you wish to include, but not in the main body of the report where its inclusion might interrupt the flow of things. For example, if the experiment was on memory and you thought that it was important to list series of items (such as different, lengthy, word lists), these could be placed in an Appendix at the end of the report. Likewise, for a student practical, it is usual for the raw data to be listed in a table (or in a number of tables) in an Appendix. If more than one Appendix is included, these are labelled numerically (e.g. Appendix 1, Appendix 2, etc.) or alphabetically (e.g. Appendix A, Appendix B, etc.) and thus referred to in the main body of the report (e.g. "See Appendix 1 for details of the word lists used."). Each Appendix must be numbered and labelled, and a brief explanation given as to its content (e.g. "Appendix 1 consists of the raw data from both the control and experimental conditions."), and they are generically referred to as Appendices.

Remember, the more of the components (outlined in this section) you have in your practical write-up, the more credit (marks) you will be awarded. Writing empirical reports should become easier the more familiar you become with the relevant format used. It should be clear by now that each section of the report serves a particular purpose. The *Title Page* identifies the report writer and provides relevant details about the project (e.g. course/module, title of project, when the study was written up, etc.); the *Abstract* is a summary of the whole report, detailing the most important components from each of the major subsections of the report; the *Introduction* is there to present the background literature and to set the stage for the experimental hypothesis(es) that is/are to be tested; the *Method* provides full details of exactly how the study was devised and how it was carried out; the *Results* section summarises the data, looks for any trends in the data, and analyses whether these trends are significant or not (e.g. are they replicable, or just a chance occurrence?); the *Discussion* looks at what was found from the study, how these findings relate to the hypothesis(es) and background literature; considers flaws/improvements/future research paradigms, and states some conclusion(s); the *Reference* section is there to log all the primary and secondary sources of information you have cited in the report; and finally the *Appendices* are there to include other information that is relevant to the report, but which does not necessarily fit in neatly with any of the other sections.

Please bear in mind that your own initial attempts at practical write-ups may fall far short of the guidelines provided here. However, as you progress through your course, you should show improvements with regard to your report writing skills. Report writing itself should get easier with the guidance provided on courses/modules on research methods and, of course, with practice.

Please note: An example of a practical write-up can be found in Appendix 2.

CHAPTER FIVE

A guide to preparing for examinations

INTRODUCTION

An examination is an event during which the student is required to answer questions (usually set by the course tutor) under conditions which have a strict time limit imposed and during which the student is not normally allowed to refer to any external information source (i.e. books, journal articles, notebooks). There are some exceptions to this. One is where you might be allowed to use a calculator and/or a statistics book in an exam that involves statistical analyses. A second is where you have what is known as an *open book* exam. An open book exam is where the student is allowed to take lecture/revision notes relevant to that topic (say Developmental Psychology) into the exam room, and sometimes the student can take in related literature (e.g. books). However, with an open book exam, the student will not normally be allowed to see the examination paper beforehand and their work will be marked using more stringent criteria than for an unseen exam. Where courses run open book exams, the module/course tutor will provide specific guidelines on how such an assessment is implemented.

Some examinations are *seen*, which means that the student has previous knowledge of the exam questions, whereas the majority of exams on psychology undergraduate courses are *unseen*, which means the student does not have access to the questions on the set exam paper. The marking scheme for a seen exam will be different from that for an unseen exam, the former being marked using more stringent criteria than the latter. There is one other type of exam that students may come across, where a *multiple-choice* questionnaire is used. A multiple-choice exam paper usually consists of a series of short questions (e.g. 50–100 questions) with each question having four or five possible answers. The aim is to choose the correct answer for each question. Wrong answers can be penalised by deduction of a fraction of a mark (say, a quarter of a mark) for each incorrect answer. The precise format and rules governing multiple-choice question papers should be available on request from your course tutor.

The majority of exam papers conform to the type wherein a series of questions are posed and the student is required to select two or three to answer within a set period of time (typically either two or three hours). The answers are usually in the form of short essays. The keywords likely to appear in examination questions are the same as those outlined in Chapter 3.

Why do most psychology courses have an examination component?

Exams are seen as a way of testing what you have learned over several months on a particular course. You have to prepare revision material, retain the information, and finally, use that information to answer questions in the examination. Indeed, many employers are impressed by exams and will ask you to list your exam grades on a job application form or curriculum vitae (cv).

Exams are seen by many as being a fair comparison of different people's abilities. This is because an exam reflects what you can produce on your own, under strictly supervised conditions, and working to a time limit. Indeed, some students appear to be strong at exams and weak at coursework, and some students vice versa, so having exams is seen by many tutors as a fair way of treating students. Whatever your views on how fair, comparable, or useful exams are as a learning tool, it appears that they are here to stay.

What you will find is that, if you are well prepared for an exam, it provides you with some sense of comfort and helps to reduce the anticipatory anxiety associated with exams (at least that's the theory!). So, what preparation can be done for an exam?

REVISING FOR THE EXAMINATION

Revision session given by the tutor

Most tutors are more than willing to give students some form of revision session (or advice about revision) leading up to the examination. This may be built into the course timetable itself, with (ideally) at least one week being allocated to self-directed revision on the part of the student. Please note that some institutes, or individual tutors, may have a different approach to revision than that outlined here. A formal revision session might involve the student being given the following information:

- An overview of main areas covered
- An exposition of the format the exam will take (e.g. Is it a multiple-choice exam or essay-type questions? What time limit has been set for the exam? etc.)
- Either a copy of a past exam paper or instructions on where to find the past exam papers (usually located in the Library)
- Advice on how best to handle the revision process (some tutors may refuse to give advice on this, in the belief that it is your responsibility)
- Answer any questions the students have

The amount of guidance given by a tutor about revision will obviously vary from tutor to tutor. You must be prepared to go to the tutor and (politely) request further advice about what to expect (and even how best to revise) for a particular exam if you feel unsure about the whole process. This advice can be essential if you are not used to sitting exams (as is the case, for example, with some mature students just returning to education). Remember, it is no good complaining about the lack of advice *after* the event.

Revision carried out by the student

Having suggested the potential role of the tutor in the preparation process, it is necessary to consider the role of the student—who must ultimately take responsibility for preparing for impending exams.

Things you must do when preparing for examinations
- Attend all revision sessions and take note of what the tutor says
- Clarify any points (or areas to cover) if you are unclear
- Look at past exam papers: see what the format is likely to be
- Put together a set of revision notes, with brief supporting references (e.g. A. Freud, 1936; Seligman, 1992) in relevant parts of text. Remember, you are not expected to provide a full reference section in an exam
- Leave sufficient time for revising your notes (e.g. 3–4 days)

Organising material for revision

The key to successful revision is to *organise* your revision material. You can do this by:

- Setting aside several hours during which you are going to organise all of your revision notes
- Sort the information for a particular course into a hierarchy. If possible start to organise the material for a particular course as soon as possible. Indeed, many tutors would advise starting to organise the material derived from lectures from the start of the lecture programme. Organising course material into a hierarchical form can provide a powerful cue for recall at a later stage. An example of how a set of course material can be organised in this way is shown in Fig. 5.1

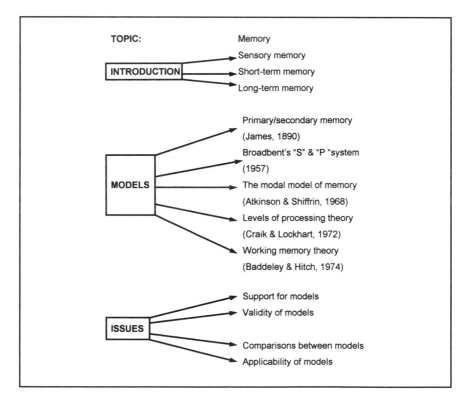

FIG. 5.1. A simple plan for organising the material for revision. You can begin by organising the course material into overall headings (in bold) and subheadings.

Such a strategy is flexible enough to allow for most questions on this particular topic to be addressed (e.g. "Describe working memory.", "Compare and contrast working memory and ...", "Discuss how useful working memory is ...", "How has working memory been applied?", and so on). When organising material for revision, look for relationships between the subsets of material. Organising the material at the encoding stage should improve the subsequent retrieval of that material (see e.g. Atkinson et al., 1996, Chapter 8).

It is important to note that if you do decide to adopt this approach to revision, it may well take you most (if not all) of your first year before you can implement it effectively. However, if you practice using such techniques during your first year, you should see the benefits during the two final years of the course. (And remember, for most undergraduate degree courses in psychology it is the two final years that determine your degree classification.) Another possible strategy is to sort the information into some kind of "story" with a beginning, middle, and end. Whatever specific strategy you use, it is always best if it is you who selects the strategy and organises the material according to that strategy.

Facilitating memory of the material
When revising the material, many people find that reciting the material over and over again helps to consolidate it (i.e. transferring it to long-term memory). However, as pointed out in Chapter 2, actively learning the material can provide a powerful framework and strong memory trace. When revising try to:

- Organise the material into some overall framework, based around the major issues and/or debates raised on the course itself, possibly using some organisation similar to that shown in Fig. 5.1 previously
- Use techniques that enable you to condense the material into manageable forms
- Critically analyse the material and pose questions about the material which you believe are important to the area covered
- Consider how the material compares with, or relates to, other issues/areas covered on the course
- Think about the strengths and weaknesses of the literature

Context can also have an effect on remembering: revising in the same room that you will subsequently take the test can be useful—the "cues" in the study setting can act as "memory triggers" that can facilitate remembering. Some researchers go as far as to suggest that chewing the same flavoured gum in the exam, that you have used during revision, can act as a memory aid! (Quinn, 1995)—but I don't recommend this as your main revision strategy.

Revising the material

Revise in short bursts rather than one long session. Stagger your revision sessions (e.g. do a 1–2-hour revision session, then take a break, and repeat the process once or twice more during the day). Testing and re-testing yourself on the material you are revising can also be of help (e.g. going over a particular point, or reference, can aid consolidation). Some people revise using a whole range of senses; thus, some people form mental images of the information, or as mentioned earlier, put the whole argument into some story form. Again, if you think it might help, "read it, write it, say it, sing it, and imagine it" (Lengefeld, 1987). Finally, *make sure you have covered enough topics in your revision of the area to pass the exam*: aim to revise at least one more topic than is minimally required (e.g. revise four areas instead of the three needed to cover the number of questions likely to appear on the exam paper). Question spotting and restricting your revision to the bare minimum number of areas is *not* recommended as a strategy. See also Acres (1987) and Lengefeld (1987) for good general advice on study skills strategies and exams.

Carrying out a "mock" examination

A very useful strategy for testing how well you have learned the material would be to have a "mock exam", during which you try to answer a number of questions from a past paper within the time limit set for the exam. This is a highly recommended strategy, which will be the closest you are likely to come to the real thing. Of course, preparing revision notes can be made easier if you work as part of a small group. This can alleviate some of the boredom brought about by many long hours of revision. Getting together with a few fellow students and going through a "mock exam" is also a very good idea because not only should it alleviate some of the tedium of working alone (although it is acknowledged here that some people like to work alone), but you can look at each other's work and provide feedback. If you do decide to work as part of a group, make sure the work (for example, collating revision notes) is allocated on an even basis and that your fellow students are turning up at the agreed times. Also make sure that your final revision notes, examples of answers, etc., are your own individual interpretations of the literature.

Things to avoid when preparing for examinations
- Do not leave your revision until the last minute (e.g. the day before)
- Do not just rely on past papers, hoping the questions will be the same
- Do not rely on the hearsay of other students. If you want to know something, ask your tutor (the worst she or he can say is "no")
- Do not go on a drinking session the night before an exam: alcohol can act to dull your memory
- Try not to eat a heavy meal before an exam; it can make you feel drowsy and lethargic
- Try not to get involved in any group hysteria immediately before going into the exam (at that stage it's impossible to change things)

TAKING THE EXAMINATION

Having considered what exams are and how one might prepare for them, it is logical to consider what strategy one can adopt during the exam itself. People can behave quite erratically under times of stress. Having a plan of action might help to overcome the panic, and related erratic behaviour, which some people experience in the exam room. What follows are some guidelines on how to take the exam itself. Again, it is stressed that you may well choose to adopt a modified approach to the one proposed here. When you are seated in the exam, make sure you have all the necessary things with you at the desk. Check that you have the right examination paper in front of you (some exams have several subjects sitting at the same time). The invigilator will announce the start of the examination and any other relevant details (such as the rules of conduct). Remember, if you need to gain the attention of the invigilator, raise your hand as a signal and one of the invigilators will attend to you. Once the exam has started, the first 10 minutes or so are crucial: in this time you can organise yourself so that the remainder of the time can be spent concentrating on getting your arguments (with supporting references) down on paper. So, what should be done within this first 10 minutes or so?

- Take a few minutes reading through all the questions on offer. Make sure you are aware of any specific requirements on the paper. For example, some papers have a compulsory question in Part A and a choice from those questions in Part B; or require you to answer so many questions from each section on the paper

- Make sure you know how many questions you need to answer
- Ensure that you allocate an equal amount of time per question (unless the exam paper states otherwise)
- Decide which questions you are going to answer (perhaps base your choice on how familiar you are with the background literature for that particular topic)
- Perhaps draw up a plan for each question. This might include jotting down the main points and references for each topic; for some, this might offer a structure around which an essay can be organised. It is acknowledged here that some people don't use plans. In fact, research shows that producing essay plans in exams does not lead to higher grades (Norton & Hartley, 1986). If you do choose to use plans in the examination context, each plan could be a modified version of the hierarchy used in the revision stage (e.g. in Fig. 5.1). For example, see Fig. 5.2 below.

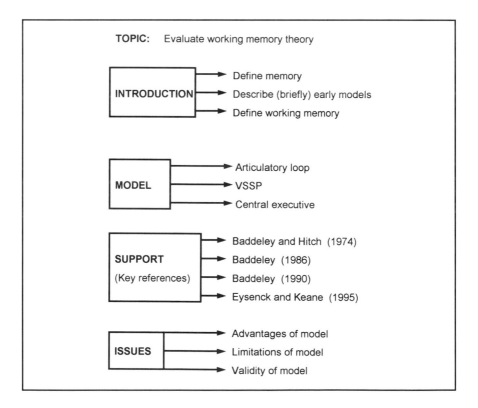

FIG. 5.2. Constructing an essay plan: this simple essay plan could help when organising material for a particular topic (e.g. working memory theory).

- Keep a check on the time: you'll be surprised how quickly it goes
- Make sure each answer has a coherent structure to it; that it *actually answers the question* set; and reaches some conclusion(s)

What are the main components of a good answer likely to be?
A general format for a good exam answer is one that:

1. Has an opening paragraph explaining what the question is asking and how (put briefly) you are going to answer it.
2. Defines any important terms contained within the question.
3. Attempts to answer the question posed in the title.
4. Presents and interprets relevant theory and research in support of the relevant concept(s), but also presents literature which is critical of that concept. Try to include up-to-date literature in addition to relevant historical theory and/or research; this will, of course, depend on the nature of the question set; that is, whether you are asked to describe, discuss, evaluate, etc..
5. Has a good structure, with each new section flowing from the previous one.
6. Shows interpretation and critical awareness of the literature wherever possible.
7. Draws the essay to a close by stating what conclusion(s) (if any) can be drawn from the discussion/evaluation of the literature.

Please note: If you think your tutor has a preference for a format that may differ from the above, check with her or him beforehand.

Finally, if you run out of time on a particular essay indicate this on your script (and perhaps make some brief notes with reference to the points/literature you would have discussed). Only by doing this will your tutor realise that you have run out of time, and may show some leniency when marking the script.

After the examination

After taking the exam, try to avoid the usual post-mortem that always seems to follow immediately after such an event. There is no point in going through what you did or did not do during the exam—you *cannot* change things at this stage. If you do start to compare your experience in the exam with another student's experience, you will probably start having doubts (often unfounded) about your own performance, which will only interfere with any further revision you have to do.

FAILING AN EXAMINATION

The majority of students (provided they have revised well) will pass their exams the first time round. However, if you fail an exam, most courses allow you to resit. If this happens, you will be asked to resit at a later date and you should seek further advice from your tutor. Explain to the tutor what you did in that first exam and try to establish where improvements can be made. (The tutor will not tell you what to write about, but can provide some general advice on how to improve your technique.) If you do find yourself in the position of having failed a resit, then seek advice from your tutor about what procedures are in place at your institute to deal with this.

Please note: Two examples of completed exam questions are provided in Appendix 3 and should be consulted in conjunction with the information provided here.

The final section of this chapter provides guidelines as to what constitutes an answer in a particular class or range of marks (for example, a first-class answer). These guidelines apply to coursework and examination essays.

GUIDELINES ON CATEGORIES TYPICALLY ASSIGNED TO ESSAYS

Although academic institutes will differ to some extent about what constitutes a particular mark/class assigned to an essay, the following guidelines will more or less be adhered to in most institutes. Check the precise percentage range for each category used in your own department/section, as there are variations in these across institutes. In addition to these components, marks may be gained or lost depending on how legible, neat, and comprehensible your essay appears to the marker.

A first-class mark (usually 70% upwards)
A first-class essay is one that incorporates the following:

- Clearly and fully addresses topic/essay question
- States the structure at the beginning and adheres to that structure
- Shows integration of a range of materials
- Flows from one argument to another

- Provides theoretical and/or empirical support where relevant
- Shows critical evaluation of relevant theory/research
- Demonstrates originality in the writing
- Brings essay to a close with some good conclusion(s) about topic

As you move through the years (from first year, to second year, and so on) you will be expected to show evidence of having read more primary source material; e.g. journal articles. (See Chapter 3 for further details on the distinction between primary and secondary sources.) The more of these components you have in your essay, the higher your mark will be within the first-class category.

An upper second-class (usually 60-69%)
A typical upper second-class answer will incorporate the following:

- Makes a clear attempt to address/answer the essay question or topic set out in the title
- Has a fairly well-organised structure that is adhered to throughout most of the essay
- Flows from one statement to the next, from one argument to the next
- Provides theoretical and/or empirical support where relevant, but less coverage of primary sources than found in a first-class answer
- Shows some critical evaluation of relevant theory/research
- Draws some conclusion(s) from the literature presented

A lower second-class (usually 50-59%)
A typical lower second-class answer will incorporate the following:

- Presents material relevant to the topic, and attempts to answer the essay question or address the topic well
- May have elements of a structure to it, but this structure is loose and does not flow from statement to statement, or from argument to argument
- Has a weak line of argument; many arguments will be based on little supporting evidence
- Will cite sources (mainly book references) which come from the main reading list provided in lectures or from the course outline
- Shows little (if any) evaluation of the material
- Makes many unsupported claims
- Reaches weak (if any) conclusion(s)

A third-class (usually 40-49%)

A typical third-class answer will incorporate the following:

- Makes some attempt to answer the question/address the topic
- Has no clear structure to the essay
- Makes unfounded assertions
- Presents no clear relationship between lines of arguments
- Has many obvious omissions
- Has some, but very little, supporting evidence for claims made in essay
- Fails to reach any conclusion(s)

Pass grade

Some institutes have a pass grade to indicate work that has narrowly missed the fail category (e.g. 39%). The pass grade essay will approximate the following:

- Loosely attempts to answer question, but has many errors/omissions
- Includes some related psychological content, but without it paying enough attention to detail
- Has little structure and is badly organised
- Has no coherent flow of arguments, or theme running through essay
- Provides little (if any) support
- Provides no sensible conclusion(s)

Fail

An essay given a fail mark is likely to:

- Fail to answer question set or address topic
- Have no detectable structure or framework
- Comprise a set of statements that do not relate to each other
- Lack any line of argument
- Fail to support claims made with any sources
- Have no conclusion(s)

CHAPTER SIX

After the degree: Opportunities for a graduate of psychology

INTRODUCTION

Having completed an undergraduate degree in psychology, the next step is to decide what to do afterwards. Some psychology students go on to do further training in psychology or a related area. Some go on to carry out psychological research, whereas others will do other things (e.g. teach on psychology courses, applied psychology). However, many students use their graduate status to obtain jobs in fields far removed from the formal topics covered on their psychology courses. For example, one student might apply for a job in personnel work, another might apply for a managerial role, whilst another still might enter onto a conversion course and completely change their focus (conversion courses to other fields, such as law, are not uncommon). In addition, a number of graduates decide to work or engage in further study abroad.

The Association of Graduate Careers Advisory Service (AGCAS) (1996) have produced statistics on first destinations of psychology graduates. These reveal the following:

- 44.6% of psychology graduates obtained permanent employment in the UK
- 8% obtained short-term employment in the UK
- 1.9% obtained overseas employment
- 13.9% went on to further academic study
- 6.7% went on to teacher training

- 5.7% went on to some other form of training
- 3% comprised overseas students leaving the UK
- 9.4% were registered as unemployed
- 6.8% were not available

(*Source: What graduates do*. The Association of Graduate Careers Advisory Service [AGCAS], 1996b.)

For some useful guidance on working or studying abroad, as well as contact addresses, see, for example, the booklet titled *Careers: Work and study abroad*. This document is published by AGCAS (1996a) and a copy should be available from your Careers Service on campus. Whatever you decide to do as a graduate, a number of things are clear:

- Being a graduate increases your chances of finding employment (seek advice from your Careers Advisory Service).
- Because psychology is a subject that entails so many topics that can relate to everyday life (e.g. group dynamics; assessing people; attempting to understand human motivation, etc.), it will have something in common with the majority of careers that graduates are likely to pursue.

Therefore, having a degree in psychology is likely to be seen in a positive light by a potential employer. The aim of this chapter is to provide advice on some of the opportunities open to a graduate of psychology. *These opportunities should be considered sooner (early in your final year) rather than later.* The Careers Services within your institute can provide good guidance about future potential careers for graduates.

GRADUATE STATUS

Attaining a Bachelor's degree in psychology means that the recipient has gained a good, *general* grounding in psychology. These can be BA (Bachelor of Arts) or BSc (Bachelor of Science) degrees. The major difference between the two types is the amount of scientific content included on the course (such as research methods, statistics, biological emphases, etc.). Most psychology degree courses are of the BSc type. Obtaining a Bachelor's degree in psychology means that you have gained an all-round, but basic, knowledge of psychology (which is why you study so many topics on a psychology course). This is important, because it means that to *specialise* in an area of psychology you must undergo further training in an applied area, or take some form of postgraduate course (for example, an MSc in Occupational Psychology). You can specialise in psychology via a number of routes, such as postgraduate training or research, or applied psychology courses—both routes are considered here.

POSTGRADUATE TRAINING AND RESEARCH

Postgraduate degree courses fall mainly into two categories (there are exceptions to this; e.g. Postgraduate certificates or diplomas), a Master's degree and a Doctorate (or PhD). So, what's the difference?

Traditionally, a Master's degree meant that on completion of the degree you were qualified to practice in a particular area of psychology. Currently, the possession of a Master's degree indicates that you have advanced knowledge in a specialist area of psychology. This is still true today—many institutes run MScs in Counselling Psychology, Educational Psychology, Occupational Psychology, and so on. However, with most specialisms in psychology, experience in a related aspect is required in addition to the relevant undergraduate and postgraduate qualifications. For example, to become an Educational Psychologist a person must attain a good undergraduate degree qualification, a relevant teacher-training postgraduate qualification, as well as teaching experience and the postgraduate qualification in Educational Psychology itself. Historically, being in possession of a PhD meant that you were qualified to teach at a university. Currently, the completion of a PhD indicates that the recipient has a full, specialist knowledge of a particular area of the discipline and that this knowledge of the subject extends right up to the boundaries of current theory and research (Phillips & Pugh, 1995). The PhD is the highest degree awarded by a university. It means that the holder is an authority on a particular area (e.g. on, say, schizophrenia), and that she or he is a fully professional researcher within that field; i.e. that she or he has developed advanced researching skills related to the subject specialism.

Funding for Master's and PhD courses is normally secured by the university or institute advertising such places. For example, a university might receive funding from one of the major research funding bodies, such as the Economic and Social Research Council, the Medical Research Council, or some other source. Normally a student on one of these courses will have all their university fees and costs paid, and usually receives some form of maintenance grant. The size of the grant may vary, but is typically in the region of four or five thousand pounds per year, and could be more if it is a studentship that requires the student to teach as part of their contract (e.g. as a practical demonstrator; running seminar classes, etc.). In addition, students can earn extra cash by taking on some academic duties at the university itself (such as marking scripts). Normally, the funding for a PhD will include some (limited) funds for travelling to conferences both at home and abroad, where you can present some of your research findings. In addition to this, many people undertake Master's and PhD degree courses on a part-time basis, and in many cases operate on a self-funding basis. Anyone interested in either of these two modes of study should contact the relevant university/institute to find out more about the costs/procedures involved. See: Research Opportunities, *The Times Higher Education Supplement*, February 22, 1996, for a list of universities and names of people to contact for further information on postgraduate research opportunities.

Undertaking a Master's or PhD course of study requires a great deal of commitment and hard work on the part of the individual. In many cases, studying for a PhD will involve you pursuing a particular line of research—unlike an undergraduate course, where you are taught as part of a large class. For some people this can be a daunting task. However, being awarded a higher degree like a PhD can bring with it a feeling of individual achievement quite unlike that which is experienced at any other level of study. Attaining PhD status also brings with it recognition and academic credibility within your discipline (see Phillips & Pugh, 1995, for some excellent insights into the whole process of PhD study). For further information on postgraduate studies (taught and research-based), a list of the institutes which run these courses, the facilities available, and funding aspects, see Colley (1995), Hobson's (1996) *Postgrad: The magazine*—a copy of which should be available from the Careers Services on your campus. See also *The Psychologist*— "How employers see Psychologists", 1991; "Student special issue", 1994; and "A day in the life of a PhD student" 1995, issues—for some useful insights into careers in psychology, postgraduate study, researching, funding aspects, and what it's like to be a PhD student.

APPLIED PSYCHOLOGY

Applied psychology refers to the application of theoretical and methodological advancements made in psychology to the study of practical aspects and problems experienced in everyday life. Over the years a number of applied areas have developed into distinct subdivisions, or specialisms, within psychology. These specialisms are accredited by the British Psychological Society, and it is therefore appropriate to elaborate on three different kinds of status within the Society before going on to consider these specialisms in greater detail.

Student subscribers, graduate members, and the graduate basis for registration

A *student subscriber* is someone who is registered with the British Psychological Society (BPS) and is taking a psychology course that is within the United Kingdom and is recognised by the BPS. There are other routes open to registration as a student subscriber (for these details, contact the BPS directly). Being a student subscriber means that you are a member of the Society and that you will be sent a monthly publication of *The Psychologist*, which also contains the Appointments Memorandum—within which professional psychology posts/jobs are advertised. Once you have completed your Society-accredited degree in psychology, you become eligible to register as a *graduate member*, which again means that you will be sent the relevant literature produced by the Society.

In order to become eligible for postgraduate training in psychology (e.g. to train to become a Clinical Psychologist, or an Educational Psychologist) you must be eligible for the *Graduate Basis for Registration* (or GBR). In order to be eligible for GBR you must have a relevant qualification in psychology from a UK institute that has been Society-accredited to confer GBR status: a point that is worth checking with your own institute as soon as possible. If you are not eligible for GBR then you can take a qualifying exam (contact the BPS for details on this). *It is important that your course has been Society-accredited for GBR if you are thinking of going on to specialise in psychology* (e.g. if you wish to become a Clinical Psychologist).

The major specialisms in psychology are briefly considered here. These include: Clinical Psychology, Educational Psychology, Occupational or Organisational Psychology, Criminological or Forensic Psychology, and, more recent in terms of their development, Health Psychology and Sports Psychology. See Colley (1995) for a compendium of taught and research courses in the UK and Ireland: this document contains a full list of postgraduate courses, details of facilities at particular institutes, and details on financial support. Also, write to the British Psychological Society, St Andrew's House, 48 Princess Road East, Leicester, LE1 7DR, UK for further details on particular specialisms in psychology. The BPS can also supply you with lists of accredited postgraduate courses and a copy of their *Careers in psychology* booklet (BPS, 1996). Your campus library should also have sections dedicated to literature on the various specialisms in psychology. Also, you can write to the BPS for details on registration qualifications and further training, pay scales, and prospects and conditions for each of these specialisms.

CLINICAL PSYCHOLOGY

A Clinical Psychologist interviews and provides therapeutic intervention to those people who suffer from a range of physical impairments and psychological disturbances. These disturbances can include clients who suffer from irrational fears, depression, schizophrenia, etc., or people suffering from severe learning difficulties. In addition, a Clinical Psychologist can be actively engaged in the general health field practising a variety of techniques, such as relaxation therapy, working with the elderly, and so on. They usually work either on a one-to-one basis with a client, or with groups of clients. They can operate from any of a number of places, such as a hospital, a health centre, or may visit a client at home. More often than not, the Clinical Psychologist will form part of a wider clinical team working together for the benefit of the patient; for example, with a psychiatrist, hospital staff, social workers, etc. The majority of psychologists in this field operate within the National Health Service, but a minority go on to private practice. Many are engaged in research in addition to their other duties.

Training to become a Clinical Psychologist involves postgraduate training at PhD level (Doctoral programme)—referred to as a Doctorate in Clinical Psychology, also known as DClin courses. (Note that the majority of these courses have recently changed from MSc to PhD status.) These are mostly full-time courses which take 3 years to complete, they recruit each year, and normally require a first-class or upper second-class psychology undergraduate degree as a minimum entry requirement. This undergraduate degree must be accredited by the British Psychological Society (BPS). Competition for places on such courses is very high (with approximately 20 applicants considered per place on a course)—so getting the best possible degree classification is essential. The specific aim of such a course is to provide essential knowledge and training in the following areas: assessment, treatment/intervention, research, professional conduct, management and teaching, related to clinical psychology. Typically, each course will have several funded places and sometimes a few self-funded places (where the applicant is responsible for arranging their own financial support, payment of course fees, etc.). Applications for clinical psychology courses are processed via the Clearing House Scheme. A copy of the *Postgraduate Courses in Clinical Psychology Handbook* can be obtained from the Clearing House for Postgraduate Courses in Clinical Psychology, University of Leeds, 15 Hyde Terrace, Leeds LS2 9LT; there is a small charge for the application. A specific timetable of deadlines is in the handbook.

Once you have completed the relevant postgraduate clinical psychology course, you are then eligible to practise as a professional Clinical Psychologist, either within the Health Service, in a community service setting, or as a private practitioner. At present, availability of posts for trained Clinical Psychologists is high (and fairly high salaries can be earned soon after qualification). Many applicants who are unsuccessful on their first application go on to gain experience in the clinical field by securing a post as a Psychology Technician, or as an Assistant Psychologist. This will involve working as part of a team (perhaps based in a hospital, a special unit, or some other institute) whose role is to monitor patients suffering from psychological disturbances, as well as to implement intervention strategies, normally working under the supervision of a Clinical Psychologist.

In addition, many graduates go on to study a particular aspect or aspects of clinical psychology within a Master's or PhD programme. This will take the same form as any other postgraduate research project (see the section on postgraduate training/research) but does not constitute a licence to practise as a professional Clinical Psychologist. See, for example, R.C. Beck (1992); Gale and Chapman (1984); Van Hasselt and Hersen (1994), for useful insights into clinical psychology and related issues

EDUCATIONAL PSYCHOLOGY

An Educational Psychologist is someone who uses psychological theory and application within a range of educational settings, including schools, colleges, nurseries, special units, or even in the person's home. The Educational Psychologist will spend most of her or his time assessing children's progress, their academic needs, their emotional needs, and providing help and/or advice on a range of issues; e.g. applying techniques to improve the reading skills or writing skills of a child who has impairments in these processes. If a particular child is experiencing such difficulties, then the psychologist might advise teachers on how best to structure their teaching with the aim of enhancing the child's performance. Some Educational Psychologists work specifically with adults in the educational setting; for example, with teaching staff helping those students who experience educational difficulties. In addition, some advise on learning methods and processes, curriculum development, and other aspects of the educational setting; e.g. intervention when the child is engaging in behaviour that has an adverse effect on her or his learning (as in truancy, for example).

Most of the psychologists working in this field will be employed by local authorities, but some run private practices or act as independent consultants, and many will be engaged in research. As with many specialisms in psychology, to qualify as an Educational Psychologist one has to undergo postgraduate training, usually in the form of a 1- or 2-year Master's course in Educational Psychology—referred to as an MSc or MEd in Educational Psychology. On such a course, theoretical and practical elements are incorporated in order to equip the student with the necessary knowledge and skills to practise as an Educational Psychologist. Typically, a first degree in psychology is required (with a first-class or upper second-class grade), which is BPS accredited. To practise in England, Wales, and Northern Ireland, you also need a teaching qualification (e.g. a Postgraduate Certificate in Education), up to 2 years teaching experience with children or young adults, as well as the training at Master's level itself. This is the typical route through which people become Educational Psychologists. In Scotland, teaching experience is not required. Usually, following training, the Educational Psychologist will be required to practise under supervision for up to 1 year.

Again, once qualified and experienced, the salary level can be fairly high. See *The Psychologist*, "Education Section", 1992, for some useful discussion points on psychology and education. In addition, many graduates go on to study a particular aspect or aspects of Educational Psychology within a Master's or a PhD. This can take the same form as any other postgraduate research project (see the section on postgraduate training/research), but does not necessarily constitute a licence to practise as a professional Educational Psychologist. See, for example, Gale and Chapman (1984); Sprinthall, Sprinthall, and Oja (1993); Woolfolk (1995), for some useful insights into Educational Psychology and related topics.

OCCUPATIONAL/ORGANISATIONAL PSYCHOLOGY

An Occupational or Organisational Psychologist is one who uses specific psychological knowledge and applications within a work or business setting. This specialism is also referred to as Ergonomics, Applied Psychology, Industrial Psychology, Management Consultancy—to name but a few titles. The types of work setting an Occupational Psychologist might be in will vary, such as companies (in the private and public sectors), hospitals, prisons, government, and public services. The main role of the psychologist in this specialism is devising selection procedures for new staff—devising and carrying out tasks designed to look for particular characteristics (such as numeracy, attitudes, skills, personality) that will best suit the job. The psychologist will also be involved in monitoring existing staff performance; devising ways of improving the work setting; and addressing particular problems that arise in relation to work (for example, advising on stress in the workplace). Some psychologists work with industry to improve designs for particular work settings (for example, on aircraft design) or engage in research within the occupational setting. Many Occupational Psychologists will operate in several work settings throughout their working week and work as part of a team—often working alongside managers, training officers, trade union representatives, etc. A number of the psychologists working in this field will be engaged in research.

Training as an Occupational or Organisational Psychologist involves a first degree in psychology (first-class or upper second-class) which is BPS accredited; a 1-year full-time (2-year part-time) postgraduate Master's degree (MSc), followed by a 2-year placement, working under supervision. Competition for places on such courses is also high (within the region of eight or nine applicants considered per place). Once qualified, psychologists working in this specialism can command fairly high salaries, and can go on to become consultants in their field. See also *The Psychologist*, "Testing in the workplace", 1994, for some useful insights into issues regarding occupational psychology.

Again, many graduates go on to study a particular aspect or aspects of occupational psychology within a Master's or PhD (e.g. stress in the workplace). This will take the same form as any other postgraduate research project (see the section on postgraduate training/research), but again does not necessarily constitute a licence to practise as a professional Occupational Psychologist. See, for example, R.C. Beck (1992); Gale and Chapman (1984); Miner (1992); Robbins (1996) for some useful insights into Occupational/Organisational Psychology and related topics.

CRIMINOLOGICAL/FORENSIC PSYCHOLOGY

This specialism is also referred to as Legal Psychology Criminological Psychology generally refers to the work of those psychologists who become involved in applying psychological theory and methods to the study of many aspects of crime. For example, an experimental psychologist might carry out research on theoretical explanations of crime, looking at the role of eyewitness testimony in the legal process, evaluating the legal processes in court, or advising the police on training procedures. Over the last two decades, research has flourished in areas such as: crime detection, police selection and training, courtroom dynamics, rules of law, etc. See, for example, Colman (1995a); Feldman (1993); Hall-Williams (1984); Stephenson (1993) for good coverage of many of these aspects.

Forensic psychology specifically relates to those psychologists acting as experts who offer psychological evidence in criminal cases (as well as being involved in civil cases). The main role of a Forensic Psychologist is to gather information in relation to the trial of a suspect, the collection of evidence for appeal boards, parole boards, or tribunal hearings (Blackburn, 1993). In this respect, the role of a Forensic Psychologist is a specialist function. In addition, she or he can be involved in researching criminal behaviour, as well as with the assessment and treatment of offenders. Thus, the Forensic Psychologist is a much more specialised, focused individual whose main role is, as the term suggests, to act as an expert adviser within a legal forum. One example of the role played by a Forensic Psychologist comes from their involvement in the prediction of future criminal behaviour of convicted offenders (recidivism). This is particularly important where you have a very violent offender (such as a violent rapist). The main aim of so-called "predictions research" is to provide advice within a legal setting (such as a tribunal considering the early release of a prisoner). At such a hearing the Forensic Psychologist will give their professional opinion as to whether the prisoner is likely to re-offend and therefore pose a threat to the public (see, for example, Blackburn, 1993).

Psychologists working in these specialist fields often work in the penal system or in the National Health Service. Traditionally, many of those working as Forensic Psychologists came mainly from other specialisms (such as clinical psychology and psychiatry). However, there are a number of postgraduate courses springing up across the country (and in the USA). These courses are specifically designed to train graduates in areas such as Criminological Psychology and Forensic Psychology, or they embed psychology within the study of the criminal justice system. Such courses can be at Diploma level (1–2 years of study), or at Master's level (2–3 years of study), and can be either on a full-time or part-time basis. Funding for such courses is varied, with some courses providing accompanying grants, whereas others may be self-funded. Graduates wishing to specialise in this field should have a good first degree (preferably upper second-class or above) which is accredited by the BPS. There is a selection procedure run by the Civil Service for Basic Grade Psychologist posts for those wishing to become a Prison Psychologist.

Since Criminological Psychology/Forensic Psychology is, at present, a fast-growing area, the number of such courses is on the increase. In addition, many graduates go on to study a particular aspect or aspects of psychology and crime within a Master's or PhD (e.g. on offender profiling). Again, such projects take the same form as other postgraduate research projects (see the section on Postgraduate training/research). For additional reading on the relationship between psychology and crime see Bartol (1995); Blackburn (1993); Cooke, Baldwin, and Howison (1990); Faulk (1994); Hollin (1996). See also *The Psychologist*, "Criminological and legal psychology", 1991, for some useful insights into Criminological and Legal Psychology.

HEALTH PSYCHOLOGY

Health Psychology is the interface between psychology and medicine. More specifically, it refers to the contributions psychology makes (in terms of theory, research, and application) to the study of a range of issues pertaining to health. Some examples include: health promotion or maintenance, prevention of illness/recurrence of illness, and treatment issues. A Health Psychologist, then, is a specialist who works on a one-to-one basis with a client, or with groups of clients, on a number of medical issues. In addition, a Health Psychologist might also be involved in policy decisions related to health issues, and engage in research. Health Psychology is a relatively new specialism, and many current Health Psychologists are derived from the field of Clinical Psychology (or other health-related areas). However, specialist post-graduate courses in Health Psychology have developed recently. Such courses include training in the theoretical foundations/current knowledge of Health Psychology, research methodology, risk factors/ vulnerability factors, behaviour change, health promotion, health policy, and so on, as well as having a research project component. Often these courses will be at Master's or Diploma level, can be either full-time or part-time, and can take the form of self-funded or grant-funded courses.

As suggested earlier, on a Health Psychology course, theoretical, methodological, and treatment/intervention issues are addressed. A study of the health care system and policy, health-related behaviour and behaviour change, life stress, chronic illness, health promotion and intervention, may all be addressed at some point during the study of Health Psychology. For good insights into the topics covered in Health Psychology see, for example, Gatchel, Baum, and Krantz (1989); Kaplan, Sallis, and Patterson (1993); Niven (1994); Sarafino (1994); Taylor (1995). As with other areas, particular aspects of Health Psychology can be studied at postgraduate Master's or PhD level (e.g. the study of socio-economic status and smoking behaviour as a PhD thesis). Again, this does not necessarily constitute a licence to practise as a Health

Psychologist. The route to such courses of study, as well as issues of funding, etc., are similar to other specialisms. See also *The Psychologist*, "Health issue", 1994, for discussion of some current issues in health psychology, and "A day in the life of a health psychologist", 1993, for some useful insights into the role of a Health Psychologist.

SPORTS PSYCHOLOGY

Historically, the role of psychology in sports was one in which a sports coach might approach a psychologist for advice on particular psychological phenomena that might have an impact on their athletes' performance. Currently, the new sub-specialism of Sports Psychology represents an applied, flourishing area in which theory, research, and application are combined to address many aspects of sports and athletics. Sports Psychology, then, refers to the application of psychological theory and techniques in the sports setting, usually specifically related to athletes' performance. Indeed, much of what psychology is about—such as the study of perception, memory, imagery, motivation, personality, behaviour change, stress, group dynamics, etc.—are all of direct relevance to the sports setting. In addition to this, the sports setting offers a very good opportunity to carry out real-life research in that it provides the setting to look at psychological phenomena in the natural environment. This does not exempt the researcher from carrying out controlled, laboratory-based, experimentation into sports-related psychological phenomena.

A Sports Psychologist can be involved in a number of roles. For example, to monitor the performance of athletes, to implement psychological techniques to improve athletes' performance, as well as carrying out research in the area. It is not uncommon to find a Sports Psychologist attached to any one of a range of sporting groups, such as football clubs, athletics associations, etc. A Sports Psychologist can be heavily involved in research, perhaps gathering data on sports-related phenomena, such as the effects of psychological stress on athletes; exercise dependence syndrome, etc. A Sports Psychologist will be involved in applied aspects, such as improving motivation or mental training in sports, or focusing on other psychological characteristics, such as stress, drug dependence, burnout, etc. For good insights into theoretical concepts and applications in sports psychology see Bakker, Whiting, and van der Brug (1990); Biddle (1995); Bull (1991); Grant (1988); Williams (1993). At present, there is little in the way of taught postgraduate courses in Sports Psychology (although some do exist). Of course, individuals may study the relationship between sports and psychology at Master's or PhD level, although the availability of funded places on such a course of study is limited at present. See also *The Psychologist*, "Sport: Special issue", 1991, for some useful insights into current research in Sports Psychology.

OTHER APPLICATIONS

In addition to postgraduate research, such as Master's and Doctoral (PhD) programmes, and applied psychology, many psychologists use their knowledge/skills in other related areas. These include counselling psychologists, research psychologists, and teachers of psychology.

Counselling psychology involves counselling individuals or groups of people who experience academic, occupational, and/or psychological disturbance that is not intensive enough to warrant a serious mental disorder. In many ways, some of the duties of a therapist will overlap with that of a Clinical Psychologist. Psychologists working in this field can find themselves based in any one of a number of situations, ranging from primary health care agencies (e.g. GP surgeries) to counselling clinics, academic settings, or business organisation.

Usually, to become a Counselling Psychologist, you need a BPS accredited degree in psychology, and further training at Diploma level or Master's level—which range from 1-year to 3-year courses. For a useful discussion on a range of issues relating to counselling in Britain, see *The Psychologist*, "Counselling psychology: Special issue", 1990. See also Connor (1994); and Sanders (1996) for good insights into psychological counselling.

A research psychologist applies her or his knowledge and research skills to carry out a specific research project, the focus of which can be any one of a number of specialist areas/research focuses in psychology. The research psychologist can either devote her or his time to one particular area (for example, a research project into brain damage and memory loss), or carry out experimental research into a number of areas. Usually, such research projects are advertised through national journals or newspapers and specific details about the post can be obtained from the institute advertising the post. Such contracts are normally for a fixed term (for example, 1, 2, or 3 years) and are supported by a salary. Gaining research experience in this way can provide the graduate with invaluable experience in literature searching, and carrying out research, as well as in writing reports and journal articles. It can also lead to other opportunities. For example, if you were working at a university and another post arose (e.g. a lecturing position), you could apply for that post knowing that you have good research experience and experience of the institute itself. Research psychologists work in a variety of areas, other than an academic setting: these include working for government agencies and for private companies.

Teaching psychology can take any one of a number of forms. A graduate might take up a full- or part-time post teaching psychology. This could be in the Further Education sector; for example, teaching at a college on GCSE and A Level psychology courses, or on an Access course. Or, it could be in the Higher Education sector; for example, within a university or institute of higher education teaching on a psychology undergraduate degree course, or a Diploma course. In the university sector, there is growing pressure on those wishing to become full-time psychology lecturers to have completed (or be in the process of completing) a postgraduate course of study in psychology. Often those who apply for a post at a university will have a PhD in Psychology (or some related subject), or will obtain one in the near future. In 1991 a Diploma in the Applied Psychology of Teaching was introduced so that graduates of BPS-approved psychology degree courses could gain a BPS-accredited qualification for teaching psychology (contact the BPS for details of this course). University lecturers will teach specific areas of psychology, contribute to research within the psychology department/ section, as well as carry out related administrative duties. See Brody and Hayes (1995) for some useful insights into teaching psychology.

See also Anastasia (1964); R.C. Beck (1992); Gale and Chapman (1984); Grasha (1987); Hartley and Branthwaite (1989) for further reading on applied areas of psychology. In addition to the specialisms outlined here, many psychology graduates go on to work in a whole host of other fields. Indeed, there are good employment prospects for psychology graduates in areas such as market research, advertising, nursing, social work, sales, management posts, and so on. A degree in psychology is also seen as a good basis for future careers where further training is necessary, such as the police, the armed forces, private companies, to name but a few: see *Careers in psychology: A guide to courses and opportunities in psychology* (BPS, 1996).

PREPARING YOUR CURRICULUM VITAE (CV)

What is a curriculum vitae (cv)?

A cv should focus on particular aspects of you and your relevant life experience. The term is Latin and means (approximately) "the story of your life"—but again, it is stressed that only those details pertinent to your future career should be included: there would be little point in including a long narrative of your life. Corfield (1990) identifies six major categories that make up a cv. These comprise: personal details, details of your education, details of your employment, your interests, an additional information section, and details of two or three people who are willing to act as referees on your behalf. A summary of each category follows.

1. *Personal details:*
   - Forename and surname
   - Full address and postcode
   - Telephone number (plus any extension number)
   - Date of birth
   - Marital status, health (optional)
   - Nationality (stating if a work permit has been granted if applicable).
2. *Details of education:*
   - Starting from secondary school onwards
   - In chronological order
   - Include name of the institute, dates attended, and qualifications attained (including subjects taken and grades achieved)
3. *Details of employment:*
   - Summary of jobs/work experience
   - In reverse chronological order (i.e. most recent or current to first job)
   - Include dates, names of employers, duties involved
4. *Interests:*
   - Include physical and other activities (e.g. football, music)
   - Indicate your interests outside the work setting
     (Briefly list these as separate section or in the following section)
5. *Additional information:*
   - Include (briefly) other information relevant to the application
   - Include activities engaged in where gaps appear in your work record (e.g. travelling across America 1989-1990)
   - Brief details of final year project/dissertation
   - Any computing and word-processing skills
   - Membership of recognised association(s) (such as the British Psychological Society)
6. *References:*
   - Provide details of two or three people acting as referees
   - Provide name, title, address, telephone number, and position of employment (e.g. Head of Department)
   - Make one an academic referee who knows your work

Please note: The Additional Information section should be altered, depending upon what career/job it is you are applying for—so change this part of the cv whenever you feel that it is appropriate. Clinical psychology (used here in the sample cv) is only one of a number of specialisms that is popular with students.

Corfield's (1990) book *Preparing your own cv* provides good guidelines on putting together your own cv. It also includes several examples of completed cvs. What follows is a fictional example of a graduate version of a cv.

Example of a graduate version of a cv

Curriculum Vitae

NAME:	Thomas Smith
ADDRESS:	30, Docklands Road, Childwall, Liverpool, L12 8AP.
TELEPHONE:	0171 000 000
DATE OF BIRTH:	29.07.1962.
EDUCATION:	St. Peter & Paul's, Burgess Road, Childwall, Liverpool. 1973-1980. 5 O Levels in: Maths, English, Biology, Politics, Sociology. 2 A Levels in: Psychology (B); and Sociology (A). University of Teesside, Borough Road, Middlesbrough, Cleveland. 1993-1996. B.Sc. (Hons) Degree in Psychology (Upper second).
EMPLOYMENT:	Bloggs' Biscuit Factory, Docklands Wharf, Childwall, Liverpool. 1985-1993—Duties included plant worker; plant supervisor. Smith's Construction, Harrow Lane, Childwall, Liverpool. 1980-1985—Duties included running family building firm. Construction work.
ADDITIONAL INFORMATION:	My degree course introduced me to psychology. The course has taught me to work independently at times, as well as part of a team. It has helped me develop good organisational skills, and has greatly improved my

written and oral communication skills. I am keen to develop a career in Clinical Psychology. I have recently gained some experience working as a volunteer in a hostel for schizophrenic patients. My final year project focused on the role of memory in traumatic events and received a first-class mark (75%).

I am punctual, hardworking, friendly, and able to mix well with others. I am familiar with a number of computer software packages, including Microsoft 6 wordprocessing, SPSS for Windows, and using the InterNet. I am a student subscriber of the British Psychological Society.

I have a full, clean driving license.

INTERESTS: Reading, sports and music.

REFEREES:
1. Dr. David Paynton, Principal Lecturer in Psychology, Department of Psychology, University of Teesside, Middlesbrough, Cleveland. Telephone: 01642 000 000 ext. 0000
2. Mr. Tony Biggs, Teacher, 4 Docklands Avenue, Childwall, Liverpool. Telephone: 0171 000 000.

Some important points about the cv

- Keep it brief: about 2-3 sides of A4 paper
- Make sure all the essential details are included in it
- Make sure it is typed and adheres to a clear, coherent structure
- Ensure that your referees have a copy of the cv (otherwise they will be providing a reference based on little knowledge about you)
- Make sure your referees are "live" (i.e. they are still willing to act as referees for you and still at the addresses stated in the cv)
- Always inform your referees of an application you make
- Send a copy of your cv along with the application form
- If you have published work or have relevant consultancy work, type this out clearly on an additional page and attach it to the cv
- Update the cv periodically
- Send a covering letter with the cv and/or application form, which highlights why you have applied for the post and your suitability

Remember, your cv is the first contact you will probably have with a prospective employer (apart from your application form, where applicable), so sending a "sloppy", incomplete or incoherent cv may result in your being turned down at the first stage. See also McKee (1995) for guidance on preparing a cv. Once you have submitted your cv (and accompanying application form) to a potential employer/academic institute, it is a matter of waiting to hear whether or not you have been shortlisted and will be interviewed. If you are asked to attend an interview, it is up to you to sell yourself to the interviewer(s). For good insights into the interview process and guidance on how to improve your interview technique, see, for example, Breakwell (1990); Brown and Breakwell (1990); Hague (1993).

A final note from the author

Studying psychology can be both challenging and satisfying. The challenges include all those aspects involved in studying on a psychology course. The satisfaction comes from the knowledge gained in psychology and the ability to use that knowledge to solve problems about human behaviour.

An undergraduate degree course in psychology sets the basis for future work in the area. It provides a good grounding in psychology so that, if she or he wishes to, a student can go on to specialise in a particular part of psychology. A psychology degree can, of course, be useful when competing in the general graduate careers market. This is because, in addition to the knowledge gained on a psychology degree, the degree itself equips you with transferable skills that are welcomed by most employers.

Finally, for those who are about to graduate, good luck with your future careers—whether they be inside or outside the field of psychology.

References

A day in the life of a health psychologist. (1993, November). *The Psychologist, 6*(11).

A day in the life of a PhD student. (1995, July). *The Psychologist, 8*(7).

Acres, D. (1987). *How to pass exams without anxiety*. Plymouth,UK: Northcote House.

Agras, S., Sylvester, D., & Oliveau, D. (1969). The epidemiology of common fears and phobias. *Comprehensive Psychiatry, 10*, 151–156.

Alloy, L. B., Acocella, J., & Bootzin, R. R. (1996). *Abnormal psychology: Current perspectives* (7th ed.). New York: McGraw-Hill.

American Psychiatric Association. (1994). *Diagnostic and statistical manual for mental disorders* (4th ed.) Washington, DC: Author.

American Psychological Association. (1990). *Ethical principles of psychologists*. Washington, DC: Author.

Anastasia, A. (1964). *Fields of applied psychology*. New York: McGraw-Hill.

Aronson, E. (1994). *The social animal* (7th ed.). New York: Freeman.

Aronson, E., Ellsworth, P.C., Carlsmith, J.M., & Gonzales, M.H. (1990). *Methods of research in social psychology* (2nd ed.). New York: McGraw-Hill.

Association of Graduate Careers Advisory Service, The. (1996a). *Careers: Work and study abroad*. Sheffield, UK: Author.

Association of Graduate Careers Advisory Service, The. (1996b). *What graduates do*. Sheffield, UK: Author.

Atkinson, R. C., & Shiffrin R. M. (1968). Human memory: Proposed system and its control processes. In K.W. Spence & J.T. Spence (Eds.), *The psychology of learning and motivation: Vol. 2*. London: Academic Press.

Atkinson, R.L., Atkinson, R.C., Smith, E.E., Bem, D.J., & Hoeksema, S. (1996). *Introduction to psychology* (12th ed.). New York: Harcourt Brace.

Baddeley, A. D. (1983a). Working memory. *Philosophical Transactions of the Royal Society of London, Series B, 89*, 708–729.

Baddeley, A. D. (1983b). *Your memory: A user's guide*. Harmondsworth: Penguin.

Baddeley, A.D. (1986). *Working memory*. Oxford: Oxford University Press.

Baddeley, A.D. (1990). *Human memory: Theory and practice*. Oxford: Oxford University Press.

Baddeley, A.D., & Hitch, G.J. (1974).Working memory. In G. Bower (Ed.), *Recent advances in learning and motivation: Vol. 8*. New York: Academic Press.

Baddeley, A.D., Thomson, N., & Buchanan, M. (1975). Word length and the structure of short-term memory. *Journal of Verbal Learning and Verbal Behaviour, 14*, 575–589.

Bakker, F.C., Whiting, H.T.A., & van der Brug, H. (1990). *Sport psychology: Concepts and applications*. Chichester, UK: Wiley.

Bandura, A. (1973). *Aggression: A social learning analysis*. Englewood Cliffs, NJ: Prentice Hall.

Bandura, A. (1977). *Social learning theory*. Englewood Cliffs, NJ: Prentice Hall.

Bandura, A., Adams, N.E., & Beyer, J. (1977). Cognitive processes mediating behavioural change. *Journal of Personality and Social Psychology, 35*, 125–139.

Bandura, A., Ross, D., & Ross, S. (1961). Transmission of aggression through imitation of aggressive models. *Journal of Abnormal and Social Psychology, 63*, 575–582.

Bandura, A., Ross, D., & Ross, S. (1963). Imitation of field-mediated aggressive models. *Journal of Abnormal and Social Psychology, 66*, 3–11.

Barlow, D. H., & Hersen, M. (1987). *Single case experimental design* (2nd ed.). London: Pergamon Press.

Barnes, R. (1992). *Successful study for degrees*. London: Routledge.

Baron, R.A., & Byrne, D. (1994). *Social psychology: Understanding human interaction* (7th ed.). Boston, MA: Allyn & Bacon.

Bartol, C.R. (1995). *Criminal behaviour: A psychosocial approach* (4th ed.). Englewood Cliffs, NJ: Prentice-Hall.

Bausell, R.B. (1986). *A practical guide to conducting empirical research*. New York: Harper & Row.

Beck, A.T. (1967). *Depression: Causes and treatments*. Philadelphia, PA: University of Pennsylvania Press.

Beck, A.T. (1983). Cognitive therapy of depression: New perspectives. In P. Clayton & J. Barrett (Eds.), *Treatment of depression: Old controversies and new approaches* (pp.265–290). New York: Raven.

Beck, R.C. (1992). *Applying psychology: Critical and creative thinking* (3rd ed.). Englewood Cliffs, NJ: Prentice-Hall.

Becker, H.S. (1966). *Social problems: A modern approach*. New York: Wiley.

Berkowitz, L. (1993). *Aggression: Its causes, consequences, and control*. New York: McGraw-Hill.

Best, J.B. (1995). *Cognitive psychology* (4th ed.). St Paul, MN: West.

Biddle, J.H. (Ed.) (1995*). European perspectives on exercise and sport psychology*. Leeds, UK: Human Kinetics.

Blackburn, R. (1993). *The psychology of criminal conduct: Theory, research and practice*. Chichester, UK: Wiley.

Breakwell, G.M. (1990). *Interviewing*. London: Routledge.

Breakwell, G.M., Hammond, S., & Fife-Shaw, C. (1995). *Research methods in psychology*. London: Sage.

British Psychological Society. (1990). *Ethics in psychological research and practice*. Leicester, UK: Author.

British Psychological Society. (1996). *Careers in psychology: A guide to courses and opportunities in psychology*. UK: Author.

Broadbent, D. (1958). *Perception and communication*. London: Pergamon Press.

Brody, R., & Hayes, N. (1995). *Teaching introductory psychology*. Hove, UK: Lawrence Erlbaum Associates Ltd.

Brown, J.C. (1977). *Freud and the post-Freudians*. Harmondsworth: Penguin.

Brown, M., & Breakwell, G. (1990). *How to interview and be interviewed*. London: Sheldon Press.

Bryant, P., & Bradley, L. (1985). *Children's reading problems*. Oxford: Blackwell.

Bull, S.J. (1991). *Sport psychology: A self-help guide*. Marlborough, UK: Crowood Press.

Carlson, N.R. (1994). *Physiology of behaviour* (5th ed.). Boston, MA: Allyn & Bacon.

Cashdan, A., & Wright, J. (1990). Intervention strategies for backward readers in the primary school classroom. In P. Pumfrey & C. Elliott (Eds.), *Children's difficulties in reading, spelling, and writing*. London: Falmer.

Christenson, L.B. (1988). *Experimental methodology* (4th ed.). Boston, MA: Allyn & Bacon.

Clegg, F. (1990). *Simple statistics: A course book for the social sciences* (7th ed.). Cambridge: Cambridge University Press.

Colley, A. (1995). *Compendium of post-graduate studies in the UK and Ireland*. Leicester, UK: BPS.

Colman, A.M. (Ed.). (1995a). *Applications of psychology*. New York: Longman.

Colman, A.M. (Ed.). (1995b). *Psychological research methods and statistics*. New York: Longman.

Connor, M. (1994). *Training the counsellor*. London: Routledge.

Cooke, D.J., Baldwin, P.J., & Howison, J. (1990). *Psychology in prisons*. London: Routledge.

Coolican, H. (1990). *Research methods and statistics in psychology*. London: Hodder & Stoughton.

Corfield, R. (1990). *Preparing your own CV*. London: Kogan Page.

Costello, T.W., & Costello, J.T. (1992). *Abnormal psychology*. New York: HarperCollins.

Counselling psychology [Special issue]. (1990, December). *The Psychologist, 3*(12).

Cozby, P.C. (1989). *Methods in behavioural research* (2nd ed.). Mountain View, CA: Mayfield.

Craik, F.I.M., & Lockhart, R.S. (1972). Levels of processing: A framework for memory research. *Journal of Verbal Learning and Verbal Behaviour, 11*, 671–684.

Criminological and legal psychology [Special issue]. (1991, September). *The Psychologist, 4*(9).

Cronbach, L. J. (1990). *Essentials of psychological testing* (5th ed.). New York: Harper & Row.

Darwin, C. (1859). *The origin of species*. London: Macmillan.

Davison, G.C., & Neale, J.M. (1994). *Abnormal psychology* (6th ed.). New York: Wiley.

Dickman, S.J. (1990). Functional and dysfunctional impulsivity: Personality and cognitive correlates. *Journal of Personality and Social Psychology, 58*, 95–102.

Dollard, J., Doob, L.W., Miller, N.E., & Sears, R.R. (1939). *Frustration and aggression*. New Haven, CT: Yale University Press.

Donaldson, M. (1980). *Children's minds.* London: Fontana Press.

Education section [Special issue]. (1992, March). *The Psychologist, 5*(3).

Ellis, A., & Young, A.W. (1994). *Human cognitive neuropsychology.* Hove, UK: Lawrence Erlbaum Associates.

Elmes, D.G., Kantowitz, B.H., & Roediger, H.L., III. (1995). *Research methods* (5th ed.). St Paul, MN: West.

Equinox. (1992). *Born to be gay?* Channel 4, 21 February.

Eron, L.D. (1982). Parent-child interaction, television violence, and aggression in children. *American Psychologist, 37,* 197–211.

Eysenck, H.J., & Eysenck, S.B.G. (1969). *Personality structure and measurement.* London: Routledge.

Eysenck, M.W. (1994). *Perspectives on psychology.* Hove, UK: Lawrence Erlbaum Associates Ltd.

Eysenck, M.W. (1996). *Simply psychology.* Hove, UK: Psychology Press.

Eysenck, M.W., & Eysenck, M.C. (1980). Effects of processing depth, distinctiveness, and word frequency on retention. *British Journal of Psychology, 71,* 263–274.

Eysenck, M.W., & Keane, M.T. (1995). *Cognitive psychology: A student's handbook.* Hove, UK: Lawrence Erlbaum Associates Ltd.

Faulk, M. (1994). *Basic forensic psychiatry* (2nd ed.). Oxford: Blackwell Science.

Feldman, P. (1993). *The psychology of crime.* New York: Cambridge.

Ferguson, G.A. (1981). *Statistical analysis in psychology and education* (5th ed.). London: McGraw-Hill.

Fisher, S., & Greenberg, R.P. (1977). *The scientific credibility of Freud's theories and therapy.* Hemel Hempstead, UK: Harvester Wheatsheaf.

Flavell, J.H., Beach, D.R., & Chinsky, J.M. (1966). Spontaneous verbal rehearsal in a memory task as a function of age. *Child Development, 37,* 283–299.

Flavell, J.H., Miller, P.H., & Miller, S. (1993). *Cognitive development* (3rd ed.). New York: Prentice Hall.

Fransella, F. (Ed.) (1981). *Personality: Theory, measurement and research.* New York: Methuen.

Freedman, J.L. (1984). Effects of television violence on aggressiveness. *Psychological Bulletin, 96,* 227–246.

French, C.C., & Colman, A. M. (1995). *Cognitive psychology.* London: Longman.

Freud, A. (1936). *The ego and the mechanisms of defence.* New York: International Press.

Freud, S. (1912a). *Totem and taboo.* London: Routledge & Kegan Paul.

Freud, S. (1912b). Totem and taboo. In J. Strachey (Ed.), (1958) *The standard edition of the complete works of Sigmund Freud. (1958). Vol .XIII.* London: Hogarth Press.

Freud, S. (1970). *An outline of psychoanalysis* (J. Strachey, Trans.). New York: Norton. (Original work published 1940.)

Freud, S. (1974). *The ego and the id.* (J. Riviere & J. Strachey, Trans.). London: Hogarth Press. (Original work published 1927.)

Freud, S., & Breuer, J. (1955). *Studies on hysteria.* London: Hogarth Press.

Fromm, E. (1979). *To have or to be?* (2nd ed.). London: Sphere Books.

Gale, A., & Chapman, A. (Eds.). (1984*). Psychology and social problems: An introduction to applied psychology.* Chichester: Wiley.

Gardner, H. (1982). *Developmental psychology* (2nd ed.). Boston, MA: Little, Brown.

Gatchel, R.J., Baum, A., & Krantz, D.S. (1989). *An introduction to health psychology* (2nd ed.). New York: McGraw-Hill.

Glassman, W.E. (1995). *Approaches to psychology*. Milton Keynes, UK: Open University Press.

Gleitman, H. (1991). *Psychology* (3rd ed.). New York: Norton.

Grant, B.W. (1988). *The psychology of sport: Facing ones true opponent*. London: McFarland.

Grasha, A.F. (1987). *Practical applications of psychology* (3rd ed.). Boston, MA: Little, Brown.

Gravetter, F.J., & Wallnau, L.B. (1996*). Statistics for the behavioural sciences* (4th ed.). St Paul, MN: West.

Gray, A. (1979). *Pavlov*. London: Fontana.

Greene, J., & D'Oliveira, M. (1990). *Learning to use statistical tests in psychology*. Milton Keynes, UK: Open University Press.

Hague, P. (1993). *Interviewing*. London: Kogan Page.

Hall-Williams, J.E. (1984). *Criminology and criminal justice*. London: Butterworth.

Hartley, J., & Branthwaite, A. (Eds.). (1989). *The applied psychologist*. Milton Keynes, UK: Open University Press.

Haworth, J. (Ed.). (1996). *Psychological research: Innovative methods and strategies*. London: Routledge.

Hayes, N. (1994). *Foundations of psychology*. London: Routledge.

Health [Special issue]. (1994, March). *The Psychologist, 7*(3).

Heiman, G.W. (1996). *Basic statistics for the behavioural sciences* (2nd ed.). Boston, MA: Houghton Mifflin.

Hergenhan, B.R. (1992). *An introduction to the history of psychology* (2nd ed.). Belmont, CA: Wadsworth.

Highfield, R. (1994, January 19). Great brains fight for your mind. *Daily Telegraph*, 14.

Hinkle, D.E., Wiersma, W., & Jurs, S.G. (1994). *Applied statistics for the behavioural sciences* (3rd ed.). Boston, MA: Houghton Mifflin.

Hitch, G.J., Halliday, M.S., Schaafstal, A.M., & Heffernan, T.M. (1991). Speech, "inner speech", and the development of short-term memory: Effects of picture-labeling on recall. *Journal of Experimental Child Psychology, 51*, 220–234.

Hobfoll, S.E., Banerjee, P., & Britton, P. (1994). Stress resistance resources and health: A conceptual analysis. In S. Maes, H. Leventhal, & M. Johnston (Eds.), *International review of health psychology: Vol. 3*. Chichester: Wiley.

Hobsons. (1996). *Postgrad: The magazine*. UK: Author.

Hollin, C.R. (Ed.). (1996). *Working with offenders*. Chichester: Wiley.

Horgan, J. (1994, July). Can science explain consciousness? *Scientific American, 271*, 72–78.

Hothersall, D. (1990). *History of psychology* (2nd ed.). New York: McGraw-Hill.

How employers see psychologists. (1991, October). *The Psychologist, 4*(10).

Hughes, F.P., & Noppe, L.D. (1985). *Human development across the life span*. St Paul, MN: West.

Jones, J.L. (1995). *Understanding psychological science*. New York: HarperCollins.

Kail, R. (1990). *The development of memory in children* (3rd ed.). New York: Freeman.

Kantowitz, B.H., Roediger, H.L., III, & Elmes, D.G. (1994). *Experimental psychology*. St Paul, MN: West.

Kaplan, R.M. (1991). *A child's odyssey* (2nd ed.). St Paul, MN: West.

Kaplan, R.M., Sallis, J.F. Jr., & Patterson, T.L. (1993). *Health and human behaviour.* New York: McGraw-Hill.

Kazdin, A.E. (1992). *Research design in clinical psychology* (2nd ed.). Boston, MA: Allyn & Bacon.

Kimble, D., & Colman, A.M. (Eds.). (1994). *Biological aspects of behaviour.* London: Longman.

Kimmel, A.J. (1996*). Ethical issues in behavioural research: A survey.* Oxford: Blackwell.

Kingman, S. (1994, September 17). Quality control for medicine. *New Scientist, 143,* 22–26.

Laughlin, H.P. (1967). *The neuroses.* Washington, DC: Butterworth.

Lengefield, U. (1987). *Study skills strategies: How to learn more in less time.* London: Kegan-Paul.

Leyens, J.P., Camino, L., Parke, R., & Berkowitz, L. (1975). Effects of movie violence on aggression in a field setting as a function of group dominance and cohesion. *Journal of Personality and Social Psychology, 32*(2), 346–360.

Logie, R.H. (1986). Visuo-spatial processes in working memory. *Quarterly Journal of Experimental Psychology, 38A,* 229–247.

Lorenz, K. (1966). *On aggression.* New York: Harcourt, Brace & World.

Malim, T., Birch, A., & Wadeley, A. (1992). *Perspectives in psychology.* Basingstoke, UK: Macmillan.

Marks, I.M. (1969). *Fears and phobias.* New York: Academic Press.

Marshall, L., & Rowland, F. (1993). *A guide to learning independently* (2nd ed.). Milton Keynes, UK: Open University Press.

Mason, J. (1996). *Qualitative researching.* London: Sage.

McCarthy, R.A., & Warrington, E.K. (1990). *Cognitive neuropsychology: A clinical introduction.* Cambridge, UK: Academic Press.

McKay, M. (1996). The Neale analysis of reading ability revised: Systematically biased? *British Journal of Educational Psychology, 66,* 259–266.

McKee, P. (1995). *How to write a CV that works.* Plymouth, UK: How To Books.

McShane, J. (1991). *Cognitive development: An information processing approach.* London: Blackwell.

Miller, G.A. (1956). The magic number seven, plus or minus two: Some limits on our capacity for processing information. *Psychological Review, 63,* 81–93.

Miner, J.B. (1992). *Industrial organizational psychology.* New York: McGraw-Hill.

Myers, D.G. (1993). *Social psychology* (4th ed.). New York: McGraw-Hill.

Niven, N. (1994). *Health psychology: An introduction for nurses and other health care professionals.* Edinburgh: Churchill Livingstone.

Northedge, A. (1990). *The good study guide.* Oxford: Oxford University Press.

Norton, L.S. (1990). Essay-writing: What really counts? *Higher Education, 20,* 411–442.

Norton, L.S., & Hartley, J. (1986). What factors contribute to good examination marks? The role of notetaking in subsequent examination performance. *Higher Education, 15,* 355–371.

Oppenheim, A.N. (1992). *Questionnaire design, interviewing and attitude measurement.* London: Pinter Publishers.

Ornstein, P.A., Naus, M.J., & Liberty, C. (1975). Rehearsal and organizational processes in children's memory. *Child Development, 26,* 818–830.

Paivio, A. (1979). *Imagery and verbal processes.* Hillsdale, NJ: Lawrence Erlbaum Associates.

Paivio, A. (1983). *Imagery and verbal processes* (2nd ed.). Hillsdale, NJ: Lawrence Erlbaum Associates.

Parkin, A.J. (1993). *Memory: Phenomena, experiment, and theory.* Oxford: Blackwell.

Phillips, E.M., & Pugh. D.S. (1995). *How to get a PhD* (2nd ed.). Milton Keynes, UK: Open University Press.

Piaget, J., & Inhelder, B. (1973). *Memory and intelligence.* London: Routledge & Kegan Paul.

Pinel, J.P.J. (1996). *Biopsychology* (3rd ed.). Boston, MA: Allyn & Bacon.

Polermo, D.S., & Molfese, D.L. (1972). Language acquisition from age 5 onward. *Psychological Bulletin, 78,* 409–428.

Quinn, V. N. (1995). *Applying psychology* (3rd ed.). New York: McGraw-Hill.

Rachman, S.J. (1976). Therapeutic modelling. In M. Felman & A. Broadhurst, (Eds.), *Theoretical and experimental bases of behaviour therapy.* Chichester, UK: Wiley.

Ramsden, P. (Ed.). (1988). *Improving learning.* London: Kogan-Page.

Research opportunities (1996, February 22). *The Times Higher Education Supplement.*

Reyna, V. F. (1985). Figure and fantasy in children's language. In M. Pressley & C.J. Brainerd Eds.), *Cognitive learning and memory in children: Progress in cognitive development research.* New York: Springer-Verlag.

Robbins, S.P. (1996). *Organizational behaviour* (7th ed.). New York: Prentice Hall.

Robson, C. (1993). *Real world research.* Oxford: Blackwell.

Robson, C. (1994). *Experiment, design and statistics in psychology.* Harmondsworth: Penguin.

Roediger, H.L. (1980). Memory metaphors in cognitive psychology. *Memory and Cognition, 8,* 231–246.

Rogers, C. (1980). *A way of being.* Booton, MA: Houghton Mifflin.

Rogers, C. (1990). Motivation in the primary years. In C. Rogers & P. Kutniok (Eds.), *The social psychology of the primary school.* London: Routledge.

Rosenhan, D.L., & Seligman, M.E.P. (1989). *Abnormal psychology* (2nd ed.). New York: Norton.

Sabini, J. (1992). *Social psychology.* New York: Freeman.

Saks, M.J., & Krupat, E. (1988). *Social psychology and its applications.* New York: Harper & Row.

Sanders, D. (1996). *Counselling for psychosomatic disorders.* London: Sage.

Sarafino, E.P. (1994). *Health psychology: Biopsychosocial interactions* (2nd ed.). New York: Wiley.

Saunders, D. (Ed.). (1994). *The complete student handbook.* Oxford: Blackwell.

Schroeder, B.A. (1992). *Human growth and development.* St Paul, MN: West.

Sears, D. O., Peplau, L. A., & Taylor, S.E. (1991). *Social psychology* (7th ed.). New York: Prentice Hall.

Seligman, M.E.P. (1992). *Helplessness on development, depression and death.* New York: Freeman.

Serling, R.J. (1986). *Curing a fear of flying.* USAIR, 12–19.

Shallice, T. (1982). Specific impairments in planning. *Philosophical Transactions of the Royal Society London, B, 298,* 199–209.

Shaughnessy, J.J., & Zechmeister, E.B. (1994). *Research methods in psychology.* New York: McGraw-Hill.

Simon, H.A. (1974). How big is a chunk? *Science, 183,* 482–488.

Smith, B., & Brown, S. (Eds.). (1995*). Research, teaching and learning in higher education.* London: Kogan Page.

Smith, M., & Smith, G. (1990). *A study skills handbook.* Oxford: Oxford University Press

Smith, R.E. (1993). *Psychology.* St Paul, MN: West.

Smyth, M.M., & Scholey, K.A. (1994). Characteristics of spatial memory span: Is there an analogy to the word length effect, based on movement time? *Quarterly Journal of Experimental Psychology, 47A,* 91–117.

Solso, R.L. & Johnson, H.H. (1994). *Experimental Psychology* (5th ed.). New York: HarperCollins.

Sport [Special issue]. (1991, April). *The Psychologist, 4*(4).

Sprinthall, R., Sprinthall, N., & Oja, S. (1993). *Educational psychology: A developmental approach* (6th ed.). New York: McGraw-Hill.

Spyridakis, J., & Standal, T. (1987). Signals in expository prose: Effects on reading comprehension. *Reading Research Quarterly, 22,* 285–298.

Squid, G.Y. (nd). The ethnography of adultery in royal clans. *Monarchy and Monarchs, 13,* 32–48.

Stephenson, G.M. (1993). *The psychology of criminal justice.* Oxford: Blackwell Science.

Sternberg, R. J. (1995*). In search of the human mind.* New York: Harcourt Brace.

Sternberg, R.J. (1996). *Cognitive psychology.* New York: Harcourt Brace.

Student special issue. (1994, October). *The Psychologist, 7*(10)

Sue, D., Sue, D., & Sue, S. (1994). *Understanding abnormal behaviour* (4th ed.). Boston, MA: Houghton Mifflin.

Taylor, S.E. (1995). *Health psychology* (3rd ed.). New York: McGraw-Hill.

Testing in the workplace [Special issue]. (1994, January). *The Psychologist, 7*(1).

Van Hasselt, V.B., & Hersen, M. (1994*). Advanced abnormal psychology.* New York: Plenum Press.

Wadeley, H. (1991). *Ethics in psychological research and practice.* Leicester, UK: BPS.

Watson, P. (1980). *War on the mind.* Harmondsworth: Penguin.

Watson, R.I., & Evans, R.B. (1991). *The great psychologists: A history of psychological thought* (5th ed.). New York: HarperCollins.

Wenar, C. (1994). *Developmental psychopathology.* New York: McGraw-Hill.

Williams, J.M. (Ed.) (1993). *Applied sports psychology: Personal growth to peak performance.* Mountain View, CA: Mayfield.

Wolpe, J. (1973). *The practice of behaviour therapy* (3rd ed.).Elmsford, NY: Pergamon Press.

Woolfolk, A.E. (1995). *Educational psychology* (6th ed.). New York: Prentice-Hall.

Zhang, G., & Simon, H.A. (1985). STM capacity for Chinese words and idioms: Chunking and acoustical loop hypotheses. *Memory and Cognition, 13,* 193–201.

Example of a completed essay (coursework)

What follows is a completed example (the final draft) of a first-year essay (coursework, as opposed to examination) which is 1500 words in length and is a first-class grade (75%). A second-year essay (level 2), and particularly a third-year essay (level 3), would be significantly longer (approximately 2 to 2,500 words in the second year, and approximately 3 to 3,500 words in the third year), would contain more primary source material (e.g. journal articles), particularly up-to-date articles, and be more discussion based. The precise nature of the essay will depend on the essay question/title.

Subject Area: Abnormal Psychology
Year: First year
Word Length: 1500 words
Title of Essay: What are anxiety disorders and how
                  can they be treated using the
                  behavioural approach?

This essay will attempt to define what is meant by "anxiety disorders", before going on to outline some of the major aspects of behavioural therapy, and finally to assess how effective behavioural therapy has been as a form of treatment for anxiety disorders.

The *Diagnostic and statistical manual of mental disorders* (4th ed.) or *DSM IV* (1994) defines anxiety disorders as a group of disorders in which anxiety and avoidance are the main symptoms. These disorders include: Panic Disorder, Generalized Anxiety Disorder, Phobic Disorders, Obsessive-Compulsive Disorder, and more recently, Post-traumatic-Stress Disorder (see also Davison & Neale, 1990). Given the limit placed on the word length, only the Phobic Disorders will be given as an example of an anxiety disorder.

A Phobic Disorder is defined as "a disrupting, fear-mediated avoidance, out of proportion to the danger posed by a particular object or situation and is recognised by the sufferer as groundless" (Davison & Neale, 1990, p.133). An example of such a fear might be when, at the mere sight of a small spider, the person's physiological state becomes over-aroused (e.g. heart rate increases, breathing becomes problematic, involuntary trembling is evident, etc.), and the person will feel the need to flee from the situation. The person is usually aware that their fear is out of proportion to the stimulus (the spider) but cannot help their feelings of fear and dread. This is typical of Phobic Disorders (see e.g. Sue, Sue, & Sue, 1994). Thus, the symptoms experienced by a phobic person include physiological symptoms (as outlined above); psychological symptoms (e.g. a feeling of loss of control; a desire to escape from the situation, etc.), and the behavioural symptoms associated with the feared thing (e.g. avoidance of the object/animal/situation).

This fear could be in relation to actual objects or animals (e.g. a spider); environmental (e.g. earthquakes; thunder, etc.); blood, injection or injury; situational (e.g. travelling in a car/train/aeroplane, heights, etc.) or some other type. The most common types include the fear of small animals, heights, being in the dark, and lightning (see e.g. Agras, Sylvester, & Oliveau, 1969). Theories of how phobias emerge vary, and include psychological models (such as the psychoanalytic perspective; behavioural ideas) as well as biological approaches (see e.g. Atkinson, Atkinson, Smith, Bem, & Hoeksema, 1996; Davison & Neale, 1990; Rosenhan & Seligman, 1989; Seligman, 1992).

An example of a phobia is an animal phobia. Animal phobias are highly focused (i.e. on a particular animal), usually begin in early childhood and are outgrown by adulthood; and they make up about 10-20% of the general class of phobias. Animal phobics more often than not are able to recall a specific event leading up to the phobia, but some cannot recall any potential "trigger" (Marks, 1969). Inanimate object phobias include an extreme fear of things such as heights, closed spaces, dirt, thunderstorms, etc. As with the previous sub-class of phobias, the symptoms are focused around one specific object. Again, as in the previous example, individuals who suffer from this sub-class of phobias are otherwise psychologically sound (i.e. do not suffer from any form of mental illness). The triggering stimulus for inanimate object phobias can be the experience of a traumatic event (Laughlin, 1967).

So what kinds of behavioural treatments are there? And how effective are these? I shall use animal phobias as an example when considering these two issues.

Behavioural therapy is based on the idea that the irrational fear and maladaptive behaviour accompanying this (e.g. avoidance) is caused by environmental factors. These factors can trigger the onset of the phobia (i.e. cause the phobia) and reinforce the phobia (i.e. keep it going). Three types of behavioural treatment are considered here: "systematic desensitisation", "flooding", and "modelling". These three approaches to treatment have the same overall goal: to change or modify the maladaptive behaviour to make it adaptive and therefore reduce the levels of fear in the individual.

Systematic desensitisation is the most commonly used behavioural therapy (see e.g. Wolpe, 1973). In this approach the patient is asked to formulate a "fear hierarchy" which is comprised of the most feared situation, to the least feared situation. Once a hierarchy is formed the patient and therapist can

work through it from least feared to most feared
scenario. The patient is taught to use relaxation
methods beforehand (e.g. the patient sits with their
eyes closed, relaxes muscles, etc.). When fully
trained in its use, relaxation can be brought about
almost automatically by the patient. The basic
assumption is that as the patient works through the
hierarchy of fears, the relaxation training will
counteract the feelings associated with the extreme
fear, and that once each stage is conquered the next
can be conquered in a similar way. This approach to
treatment can take several weeks or months before the
final, most fearful stage in the hierarchy is
reached, but is very successful (Sue et al., 1994).

Flooding is where the patient confronts the feared
stimulus by either imagining it or being in its
actual presence (e.g. confront the spider that
induces the fear), but the exposure would be
persistent so that the patient cannot avoid the
fearful stimulus. For example, a spider phobic (a
person afraid of spiders) would be put in an enclosed
space with the spider for several minutes or even
hours. The principle here is that when the patient is
forced to face their fear, that fear will subside and
the person will return to normal. Again, relaxation
training can be given to alleviate some of the
physical symptoms associated with the phobia. This
form of treatment requires great courage on the part
of the patient and is not always best suited to some
patients (e.g. if the patient has a heart condition).
Flooding, like systematic desensitisation, has a high
success rate (see Marks, 1969; Serling, 1986).

Finally, modelling can also be used as a form of
behaviour therapy. Modelling involves the copying of
behaviour from another person (the "model"). Thus,
the phobic will watch another person (who is
non-phobic) as they confront the fearful stimulus
without reacting in a maladaptive way. For example,
someone who has a spider phobia might watch the
therapist as she/he interacts with a spider stimulus
- perhaps allowing a live spider to crawl on the
therapist's hand without appearing alarmed. The idea
behind this is that the patient will see either that

the spider (or whatever the fearful stimulus is) is not harmful, or can be tolerated, and will then go on to mimic the behaviour themselves. Again, this procedure requires great courage on the part of the phobic person and a good rapport between therapist and patient. Overall, this form of therapy appears as effective as the previous two (see e.g. Bandura, Adams, & Beyer, 1977; Rachman, 1976). Once these modelling techniques are learned, the patient can practise these adaptive behaviours on their own without the need for the therapist to be there.

The underlying thing in all three therapies outlined here is the process of extinction. In all three treatments the phobic person is exposed to the feared stimulus, and this exposure is repeated and enduring. Extinction can take place because the patient is taught to relax in the presence of the fearful stimulus, and therefore reduce and extinguish the symptoms associated with phobias (see e.g. Sue et al., 1994). Although they are effective, behavioural treatments have their drawbacks and limitations. First, they are best used in combination with other forms of therapy (e.g. relaxation therapy or drug treatment). Second, it is clear that cognition plays a role in phobias - just the mere thought of a fearful object/situation can bring on a fearful response. So learning is not the only way a person develops a fearful response. Thirdly, phobias on the whole appear to be selective in their development - they are focused on certain things (like those outlined earlier in the essay). This goes against the learning principle because virtually anything you come into a negative contact with should have equal chance of developing into a phobia (e.g. knife phobias are rare even though knives are often the cause of injury). See Atkinson et al., 1996; Sue et al., 1994 for more consideration of the advantages and disadvantages in the use of behavioural methods.

So, on the whole, behavioural methods can be used to treat anxiety disorders, but they do have their limitations - not least of which is their being based on the assumption that all things are learned via the environment. Clearly, some disorders may have biological, cognitive, or even social, roots that cannot be ignored, which is why most treatments use a combined approach.

References

Agras, S., Sylvester, D., & Oliveau, D. (1969). The epidemology of common fears and phobias. *Comprehensive Psychiatry, 10*, 151-156.

American Psychiatric Association. (1994). *Diagnostic and statistical manual for mental disorders* (4th ed.) (DSM-IV). Washington, DC: Author.

Atkinson, R.L., Atkinson, R.C., Smith, E.E., Bem, D.J., & Hoeksema, S. (1996). *Introduction to psychology (12th ed.)*. New York: Harcourt Brace.

Bandura, A., Adams, N.E., & Beyer, J. (1977). Cognitive processes mediating behavioural change, *Journal of Personality and Social Psychology, 35*, 125-139.

Davison, G.C., & Neale, J.M. (1990). *Abnormal psychology (5th ed.)*. New York: Wiley.

Laughlin, H. P. (1967). *The neuroses*. Washington, DC: Butterworth.

Marks, I.M. (1969). *Fears and phobias*. New York: Academic Press.

Rachman, S.J. (1976). Therapeutic modelling. In M. Felman & A. Broadhurst (Eds.), *Theoretical and experimental bases of behaviour therapy*. Chichester: Wiley.

Rosenhan, D.L., & Seligman, M.E.P. (1989). *Abnormal psychology (2nd ed.)*. New York: Norton.

Seligman, M. E. P. (1992). *Helplessness on development of depression and death*. New York: Freeman.

Serling, R.J. (1986). *Curing a fear of flying*. USAIR, 12-19.

Sue, D., Sue, D., & Sue, S. (1991). *Understanding abnormal behaviour (4th ed.)*. New York: Houghton Mifflin.

Wolpe, J. (1973). *The practice of behaviour therapy (3rd ed.)*. Elmsford, NY: Pergamon Press.

CRITICAL EVALUATION OF ESSAY

This essay represents a first-class piece of work for a first-year coursework essay. There are a number of strengths and weaknesses in the essay that have, taken in combination, resulted in the mid-first-class assessment it achieved.

Strengths: The major strengths of the essay are:

- It has an opening paragraph stating the structure and, for the most part, it follows this structure
- It addresses the topics well
- It integrates secondary and primary sources (both early and current) fairly well into the structure of the essay
- There is a flow to the essay: from definition to classification of the neuroses covered to treatment to conclusions
- It shows critical consideration of the area
- It answers the essay question set in the essay title
- It has a very good reference section, clear and complete
- It ends with some fairly good conclusions

Weaknesses: The major weaknesses of the essay are:

- The essay adheres to a fairly standard approach to the topic/argument
- More up-to-date primary source material needed (journal articles). This would be particularly important when students reach the second and final years of their course
- More evidence needed of reading around the topic (i.e. include references from outside main lecture references): most of the primary sources cited in the essay could have been derived from one or two of the main texts for Abnormal Psychology. This is particularly important when entering the second and third year of the course
- The overall conclusions reached could have been strengthened

Please note: By improving on these weaknesses, the final mark/grade could have been improved significantly.

Example of a practical write-up

Having covered basic research methods, having briefly considered the major ethical issues in carrying out research, and having identified the major subsections of an empirical report (all in Chapter 4) it would be useful to provide a written example of a completed practical report. What follows is an example of a practical write-up of an experiment. The experiments in the first year of a course are normally tutor-led—that is, they are designed by the research methods tutor, who supplies background references and details of the method; and who may collate the data for the results, and discuss the findings with students. When progressing through to the second year, and particularly in the final year, of a degree course, the student is expected to engage more in their own literature searching, hypothesis making, design of the method, etc. —but will be given good guidance on all of these aspects by her or his tutor.

This practical write-up is a medium length (approximately 1800 words) first year undergraduate practical, and represents a good first-class grade (78%) at this level. It is stressed here that for a second-year practical, and certainly for a final-year practical, although following the same format, the write-up will be substantially longer than in the example given here. Thus, the Introduction and Discussion sections of a final-year project would be extended to include more coverage of the literature, critical discussion, etc. The format used in this example is the same as that identified in Chapter 4. However, the report writer should try to include as many aspects of the report as she or he can so that they might achieve as high a mark as possible when assessed by the tutor. Please note that for your own reports each subsection (Method, Results, and so on) should begin on a new page. Students should bear in mind that report writing is a skill that develops over time, and that their own initial attempts may fall short of the standard set out here.

Course/Module: Research Methods - Year One.
*Title of report:*Short-term memory and its development.
Type of report: A first-year practical write-up.

Abstract

The aim of this experiment was to consider how rehearsal develops with age. It was a between-subjects design: with two age groups - 5- and 11-year-olds. In one condition, all the children rehearsed words out loud (the experimental condition), in a second condition the children did not rehearse out loud (the control condition). The dependent variable was the total number of words recalled. The results showed significantly more words recalled in the experimental group in the 5-year-olds; with no difference in recall between conditions in the 11-year-olds. These results were discussed in relation to the literature.

Please note: For the Abstract section of your own report use single-line spacing and indent.

Introduction

Human memory involves some mechanism by which we encode information about the world, store that information, retaining it in the memory system, and recall that information for future use (Atkinson, Atkinson, Smith, Bem, & Hoeksema 1996). Without this ability we would not remember who we are or what we are doing. We would be living literally one moment from the next. Memory then, is a means by which we hold information for long or short periods of time - referred to as long-term and short-term memory respectively (see e.g. Atkinson & Shiffrin, 1968).

Other researchers have looked at memory in terms of "deep" and "surface" processing (Craik & Lockhart, 1972). Current views still see memory as being made up of short- and long-term systems (see e.g. Eysenck & Keane, 1995).

Much of the early research has been carried out on adults (Baddeley, 1990). Recently, work has looked at the development of memory and what processes might be involved (like rehearsal) in this development, using children as a focus (see Kail, 1990). One development is the use of rehearsal in short-term memory - with a clear difference emerging between the ages of 5 and 12 years (e.g. Flavell, Beach, & Chinsky, 1966; Ornstein, Naus, & Liberty, 1977). For example, Flavell et al. (1966) found evidence that there was an absence of rehearsal in very young children (around 5 years), but that older children (from 9 upwards) seemed to use rehearsal to remember things. This has been supported by recent research (see Kail, 1990). Rehearsal is a term used to refer to the repetition of information (like words) over and over, in order to remember that information. It appears that as they develop, children learn the advantages of using things like rehearsal to improve their memory, and by the age of 10 to 11 years they are fully aware of this process (see e.g. Flavell, Miller, & Miller, 1993). So, as children learn to use strategies like rehearsal, there are increases in the amount of information they can recall (their memory span). This seems to be the case for a range of materials, such as words, pictures, numbers, and so on (Kail, 1990). It is this aspect of memory that was the focus of the study.

The experiment here examined the effects of rehearsing aloud on short-term memory across two different age groups: 5-year-olds and 11-year-olds. If young children do not use rehearsal by themselves, then getting them to rehearse out loud should improve their recall. If older children already use some form of rehearsal to aid their memory, then there should be no benefit in their rehearsing aloud. On this basis the following hypotheses can be made.

The hypotheses

1. There will be more words recalled in the experimental condition than in the control condition in the 5-year-olds.
    The Null Hypothesis for the 5-year-olds is that there will be no difference in recall between conditions.
2. There will be no difference in recall between the experimental and control conditions in the 11-year-olds. This is, essentially, a Null Hypothesis.

Method

Design and materials

A between-subjects design was used: with two levels of age (as described earlier) and two levels of condition. A control condition (No Rehearsal Instructions) was used in which the children were not given any instructions to rehearse; and an experimental condition (Rehearse Out Loud) was used in which the children were instructed to rehearse out loud as they heard the words. The number of words correctly recalled was the dependent variable or measure. The 5-year-olds were given lists containing between 4 and 8 words, and the 11-year-olds were given lists containing between 5 and 10 words. The different ranges reflect differences in memory spans between the two age groups. The words were chosen randomly from the following list of words (cat, ear, top, key, pig, bus, boy, time, spoon, oil, leaf, ball, rug, kite, book, pen, nose, hand, bag and dog) with no repetition of a word in a given list.

Participants

Two groups of children were used. The 5-year-old group (15 boys, 17 girls) had a mean age of 5 years, 2 months (range 4.9 to 6.00 years); and the 11-year-old group (19 boys, 13 girls) had a mean age of 11 years, 3 months (range 10.2 to 11.6 years). Participants were randomly allocated to either the control or experimental group.

Procedure
Each child was tested separately and the time taken
was approximately 5 to 12 minutes. To make sure the
children were familiar with the words, each child was
told the full list and asked to repeat each word on
the list. The words were spoken to the participant by
the experimenter and item presentation was set at a
rate of one item every two seconds. The participant
was required to recall the list of words in the same
order as it was spoken by the experimenter, with the
child saying "pass" for each word she or he could not
remember in the list. In the control condition the
following instructions were used:

> 1. I will say a series of words to you. I want
> you to try and remember the words in the same
> order that I read them. Do you understand? ·
> 2. Once I have read all the words to you I
> will raise my hand (the experimenter
> demonstrates by raising one hand). Once I raise
> my hand I want you to say all the words back
> to me, in the same order that I have read them.
> Do you understand?
> 3. If you forget one or more of the words,
> then say "pass" for each word you have
> forgotten. Do you understand?

If necessary, these instructions were repeated and
simplified for the child. Instructions and procedure
for the experimental condition were the same except
each child was instructed to repeat the words out
loud as each word was spoken to her or him. The
5-year-olds began by being given a list of 4 words
and these were increased until the child began
failing on at least 50% of the list (i.e. could not
recall more than half the words on the list), the
number of words immediately below this was seen as
that child's "memory span". The same procedure was
used for the 11-year-olds. Each list presentation and
recall time took between 20 and 60 seconds, depending
on the number of words per list. After testing, each
child was thanked and any questions were answered.

Results

Recall was scored as the number of items recalled in their correct position in the list. Table A.1 consists of the means and standard deviations for the 5- and 11-year-olds. As can be seen from the table, the younger children recalled more words in the Rehearse Out Loud condition (the experimental condition), whereas the older children showed similar recall between control and experimental conditions. These trends can be seen clearly in Figs. A.1 and A.2. The standard deviations do not deviate significantly across conditions for each age group, according to the Levenes test for equal variance

TABLE A.1
Means and standard deviations under control (No Rehearsal Instructions) and experimental (Rehearse Out Loud) conditions for the 5- and 11-year-olds

Age	Control condition		Experimental condition
11 years	Mean	4.40	4.60
	Sd	(0.69)	(0.78)
5 years	Mean	3.00	4.00
	Sd	(0.81)	(0.88)

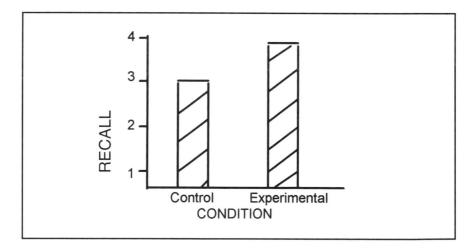

FIG. A.1. Bar graph depicting mean recall for the 5-year-olds under control and experimental conditions.

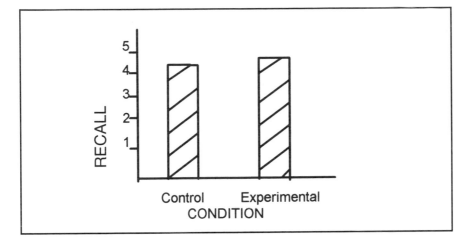

FIG A.2. Bar graph depicting mean recall for the 11-year-olds under control and experimental conditions.

(p=.519 for the 5-year-olds, and p=.30 for the 11-year-olds). In addition, overall recall is higher in the older children than in the younger children.

Independent t-tests were applied to the data. For the 5-year-olds this showed significantly more words recalled in the experimental (Rehearse Out Loud) condition than in the control (No Rehearsal Instructions) condition (t=4.5, p < .05). For the 11-year-olds there was no difference in the amount of words recalled between the control and experimental conditions (t=.80, p > .05). A third independent t-test was applied to compare all the data from the 5-year-olds with all the data for the 11-year-olds, and revealed significantly more words recalled in the older children (t=8.5, p < .05).

Discussion

The results for the 5-year-olds supported the Experimental Hypothesis set out in the Introduction (Hypothesis 1): providing young children with instructions to rehearse did lead to an increase in the amount of words they could recall. The results from the 11-year-olds were consistent with the Null Hypothesis (Hypothesis 2) set out in the Introduction: there was no difference in recall between conditions. These results can be explained in terms of the literature cited in the introductory section of this report.

These results fit in with earlier findings suggesting that very young children, in this case 5-year-olds, do not appear to use rehearsal as a means of enhancing their short-term memory capabilities (e.g. Flavell et al., 1966; Kail, 1990). However, it was shown here that when young children are encouraged to use rehearsal, as they were in the experimental condition, then this rehearsal improves their short-term memory, leading to better recall. The findings from the 11-year-olds are also consistent with earlier literature on the subject. Because they already use rehearsal, requiring them to rehearse aloud, as in the experimental condition here, had no beneficial effect on their short-term memory capabilities (Kail, 1990). In the wider sense, the findings support the notion of a short-term memory system that is used by children to encode, store, and recall information, in this case spoken words (Baddeley, 1990; Eysenck & Keane, 1995).

The experiment did have its drawbacks and there are ways of taking this research forward. For example, much of what was found here is replicating what has been found before. Future experiments should take this further, possibly by looking at a range of age groups between these two extreme ages (e.g. 7-, 8-, and 9-year-olds) to pinpoint the exact age at which rehearsal is used voluntarily. Second, although young children do not appear to use rehearsal by choice, these results do not explain why this is the case. It could be that they do not realise the potential of using such strategies (Flavell et al., 1993) or some other reason. Perhaps a future experiment could look at this from a qualitative viewpoint (e.g. ask the children questions about this).

In conclusion, the findings support the use of some type of short-term memory system in young and older children. The findings also show that young children are capable of rehearsing in such a way as to improve their short-term recall, but may not choose to do so spontaneously. Older children, on the other hand, appear more than capable of rehearsing. The experiment has alluded to ways in which this approach could be improved and extended.

References
Atkinson, R.L., Atkinson, R.C., Smith, E.E., Bem, D.J., & Hoeksema, S. (1996). *Introduction to psychology* (12th ed.). New York: Harcourt Brace.
Atkinson, R.C., & Shiffrin, R.M. (1968). Human memory: A proposed system and its control processes. In K.W. Spence & J.T. Spence (Eds.), *The psychology of learning and motivation* (Vol. 2). London: Academic Press.
Baddeley, A.D. (1990). *Human memory: Theory and practice*. Oxford: Oxford University Press.
Craik, F.I.M., & Lockhart, R.S. (1972). Levels of processing: A framework for memory research. *Journal of Verbal Learning & Verbal Behaviour, 11*, 671–684.
Eysenck, M.W., & Keane, M.T. (1995). *Cognitive psychology: A students handbook*. Hove, UK: Lawrence Erlbaum Associates.
Flavell, J.H., Beach, D.R., & Chinsky, J.M. (1966). Spontaneous verbal rehearsal in a memory task as a function of age. *Child Development, 37*, 283–299.
Flavell, J. H., Miller, P. H., & Miller, S. (1993). Cognitive development (3rd ed.). New York: Prentice Hall.
Kail, R. (1990). *The development of memory in children* (3rd ed.). New York: Freeman.
Ornstein, P.A., Naus, M.J., & Liberty, C. (1975). Rehearsal and organizational processes in children's memory. *Child Development, 26*, 818–830.

Appendices

All the raw data, computer printouts and additional materials should be placed in a set of appendices for your own report. Each appendix should be numbered, labelled, and an explanation of its contents given.

CRITICAL EVALUATION OF PRACTICAL WRITE-UP

This practical represents a good first-class piece of work for a first-year practical write-up. Although it achieved a good first-class grade, it could have been improved. There are a number of strengths and weaknesses in the practical write-up that have, taken in combination, resulted in the mark awarded.

Strengths: The major strengths of the practical write-up are:

- It follows the correct structure for a write-up of this kind
- It has a good Title Page and Abstract, which contain all the relevant details needed to convey the information in these sections
- It has a good Introduction that:
  a) Goes from the broad base to the specific focus of practical
  b) Is clear in the main focus of the experiment
  c) Contains primary and secondary sources, which are theory and research based
  d) Has coverage of the theoretical framework adopted
  e) Has a clear set of hypotheses that are to be tested
- It has a clear Method section containing all the relevant components
- It has a good Results section which covers the relevant descriptive and inferential statistics required to test the data, as well as a written interpretation of the statistics
- It has a good Discussion section which:
  a) Briefly recapitulates the main findings
  b) Relates these findings to the introductory material
  c) Has good suggestions for improvements
  d) Has some useful suggestions for future experimentation
  e) Has a good conclusion section
- It has a complete Reference section

Weaknesses: The major weaknesses of the practical write-up are:

- The main weaknesses in the Introduction are:
  a) Could have clearly stated aim of experiment at some point
  b) Needs more consideration of classic theory/research (e.g. the "multi-store" model of memory)
  c) Could have shown reading beyond the main references in this area
- The Method and Results were good—no major weaknesses to cite
- The Discussion section contains the following weaknesses:
  a) Should have given more consideration to weaknesses in the conception and design of the experiment (e.g. the fact that it is predominantly a replication of previous research)
  b) Could have included additional relevant literature

c) Could have been stronger in its conclusions (e.g. what do the findings tell us about early and current theories of short-term memory?)

Please note: By improving on these weaknesses, the final mark/grade could have been improved significantly.

Two examples of examination essays (unseen exams)

What follows are two completed examples of essays written under "mock" examination conditions. The first is an example of what one might expect at the first-year (level 1) stage, and the second comes from a second-year (level 2) piece of work. It is thought that by having both examples the reader can gain some insights into what is expected both at first-year level and beyond.

EXAMPLE 1

This sample essay is of an upper second-class standard, being awarded a mark of 64%. It represents a good first-year unseen examination answer.

Area:	Personality
Level:	Year 1: Level 1
Status:	(Unseen) Exam (part of a 2-hour paper, in which the student must answer 2 questions), following revision. hand-written answer, under invigilation

to a very disorganised behaviour pattern later in life; and if the phallic stage is not negotiated with success, then this can lead to a weak (or lack of a) conscience mechanism (Fransella, 1981).

So these stages are crucial in the forming of the adult personality - according to Freudian theory. Although the theory is interesting and has led to a number of current therapies for treating things like neurosis, the whole area does have its problems. For example, Freud's concentration on the sexual aspects of development led some to detach themselves from his work - people like Carl Jung and Alfred Adler (both around the same time as Freud). Most damaging to the theory is the fact that it cannot really be tested for validity - since Freud and his followers did not produce much in the way of "data" that could be tested (Atkinson et al., 1996). So, to conclude, Freud's ideas were useful in generating future work on personality and linking this with development, but they have been heavily criticised over the years.

CRITICAL ASSESSMENT OF EXAMPLE 1

This essay answer was given a mark of 64%. This is a good mark and reflects the incorporation of a number of those characteristics that make up a good essay—as outlined in Chapter 3. Although the essay achieved a good mark, it is necessary to point out its strengths (which enabled it to achieve the mark it did), as well as its weaknesses (which prevented it achieving a higher mark).

Strengths: the major strengths of the essay are:

- It identifies the structure of the essay
- The structure of the essay is adhered to
- There is a beginning, middle, and end to the essay
- It addresses the topic well
- It provides a selection of supporting references
- It shows critical evaluation
- It has a conclusion section to finish the essay

Weaknesses: the major weaknesses of the essay are:

- It needs more support for the claims made in the essay (preferably more primary source material)
- It could have been made clear that Freud's theory is not the only theory about the personality
- It spends too much time on description, when more time could have been spent on evaluation of the main focus of the essay
- The conclusion section is weak

Please note: Improving these weaknesses, would have improved the final mark/grade for this examination essay.

EXAMPLE 2

This sample essay is of a lower second-class standard, being awarded a mark of 57%. It represents a second-year unseen examination answer.

Area:	Cognitive Psychology: memory
Level:	Year 2: Level 2
Status:	(Unseen) Exam (part of a 2-hour paper, in which the student must answer 2 questions), following revision, hand-written answer, under invigilation

Essay Paper (Time Taken: 1 Hour)
Students must answer 1 question from this section.

1. How valid is Baddeley and Hitch's working memory model?
2. Working memory has a number of applications. Discuss.
3. Critically evaluate the working memory model.

Question 1. How valid is Baddeley and Hitch's working memory model?

Essay plan
1. Working memory defined/Baddeley and Hitch (1974).
2. Central Executive.
3. Articulatory Loop.
4. Visuo-Spatial Sketch Pad.
5. Validity - pros & cons, subsequent studies.

Essay answer
Baddeley and Hitch's (1974) working memory model
consists of three components: 1/ Central Executive –
which has a limited capacity and is the most
important component; and is used for most demanding
cognitive tasks; uses the other two components as
"slave systems" for specific purposes. 2/
Articulatory Loop – stores information phonologically
i.e. speech based, uses rehearsal, and preserves word
order. 3/ Visuo-spatial Sketch Pad – stores visual
and/or spatial information.

Articulatory loop validity
Baddeley, Thomson, and Buchanan (1975) found serial
recall was better for short words that long words.
Further studies by Baddeley et al. (1975) show that
participants' serial recall when reading out loud was
approximate to 2 seconds each word, implying that the
articulatory loop has a temporal duration, much like
a "tape loop". Baddeley et al. (1975) found that this
"word length" was eliminated with articulatory
suppression – where participants were given words
visually while repeating the numbers 1-8. This also
showed that "inner speech" or subvocal speech was
involved. This contrasts with Miller's (1956) and
Simon's (1974) chunking of units of information, as
Baddeley et al. (1975) suggests that rate of
rehearsal is important. Zhang and Simon (1985)
studied 3 Chinese materials: characters, words, and
radicals. If chunking was in force all 3 should have
the same memory span. However, recall was greatest
for characters (1-syllable words) and worst for
radicals (which were unpronounceable) – which
supports Baddeley et al. (1975).

Although word length effects are eliminated by
articulatory suppression, they weren't by visual.
Therefore Baddeley (1986; 1990) revised the
articulatory loop into a phonological loop consisting
of a) a passive phonological store concerned with
speech production and b) an articulatory process
concerned with speech perception, and having access
to the phonological store. Where auditory word
presentation gains direct access into the

phonological store; this can then gain access to the articulatory processes (e.g. rehearsal); which then feeds back into the phonological store. Visual presentation gains indirect access to the phonological store through verbal labelling (Baddeley, 1990). So, we process visual and auditory differently. The phonological loop aids in written comprehension i.e. learning to read and understand what is written.

Visuo-spatial sketch pad (VSSP) validity
Baddeley (1986, p.109) describes it as a "system well adapted to the storage of spatial information much as a pad of paper might be used by someone drawing, for example, to work out a geometric puzzle". Eysenck and Eysenck (1980) found visualisable imagery was disrupted by spatial tasks, implying that visual imagery was encoded spatially. Logie (1986) argued visual coding was important in the VSSP as disruptive line drawings needed visual as well as spatial coding. Spatial tasks are important in geographic orientation.

Central executive validity
Baddeley (1986) likened this to Shallice's (1982) supervisory attentional system with its limited capacity. It takes over demanding cognitive tasks "trouble-shooting" for less adequate systems with tasks such as problem solving. Baddeley (1984) argued that damage to frontal lobes hindered the central executive and may account for short-term memory deficits in patients where no long-term learning deficit occurred. Parkin (1993) had a patient with frontal lobe damage who had problems making complex decisions - seemingly supporting Baddeley's frontal lobe theory. The central executive may not be unitary, but may be made up of two or more components (Smyth & Scholey, 1994).

   The amount of research generated by Baddeley and Hitch's (1974) working memory model; the applications to learning to read; cognitive tasks; how we encode visually and spatially; how learning can be interrupted; applying it for a better understanding of possible effects of brain damage, all go to make it a valid theory. The central executive has not been fully explained by Baddeley and Hitch's (1974) working memory theory, and its processes are not yet fully understood. However, this alone, is not enough to make the working memory theory invalid.

CRITICAL ASSESSMENT OF EXAMPLE 2

This essay answer was given a mark of 57%. The student reported that this represented an increase in performance from the previous year (and follows her having sought advice on revision from her course tutor). It should be noted that the adoption of a particular revision strategy does not guarantee a significant improvement in grades. Performance in a particular examination can involve other factors in addition to revision; e.g. motivation, interest in a particular subject matter, how good your memory is, etc. Although the above essay achieved a good mark, it is necessary to point out its strengths (which enabled it to achieve the mark it did), as well as its weaknesses (which prevented it achieving a higher mark).

Strengths: the major strengths of the essay are:

- It identifies the structure of the essay
- The structure of the essay is adhered to
- It outlines the memory model under consideration
- It assesses each component of the model and provides support
- It has a selection of secondary and primary sources (i.e. book and journal article references), which are integrated into the structure
- The essay has a flow to it, from the opening structure to components of model to consideration of validity of model to conclusion section
- It attempts to answer the question set out in the title
- It does not contain much of the (sometimes exhaustive) waffle found in some examination essays. It concludes something about the topic under consideration

Weaknesses: the major weaknesses of the essay are:

- It lacks originality in its writing—it adheres to a fairly standard approach to the topic and uses a fairly standard set of references

- It could have had an opening paragraph, defining terms such as "memory" and suggesting how the question would be addressed
- It is lacking in detail of the sources cited, particularly the primary source material (i.e. research articles)
- The flow of the essay could be improved by having link sentences, such as: "Having now considered the articulatory loop, it is necessary to consider the other 'slave-system' known as the visuo-spatial ..."
- More could have been written about the applications of the model—which might have bolstered the argument for its validity
- Some limitations of the model should have been considered
- The conclusion section could have been strengthened

Please note: Improving these weaknesses would have improved the final mark/grade for this examination essay.

Please note also that although Example 2 appears to have more coverage of the literature, more supporting primary and secondary references, and a stronger basis for its argument than Example 1, it actually received a lower mark. This is because a student is expected to show a progression going into his or her second year (and third year). Thus, for the second-year essay to achieve the same (or greater) mark than the first-year essay, the former would have had to show a greater depth of knowledge, provide more support, more critical evaluation/discussion, and so on. Therefore, a student's marks in Year 2 can be quite different from those achieved in Year 1.

Author index

Subject index